MEANING AND READING

Pragmatics & Beyond

An Interdisciplinary Series of Language Studies

IV:3

Michel Meyer

Meaning and Reading
A Philosophical Essay on Language and Literature

MEANING AND READING

A Philosophical Essay on Language and Literature

Michel Meyer
Free University of Brussels

JOHN BENJAMINS NORTH AMERICA, INC.
One Buttonwood Square
Philadelphia, PA 19130
DISTRIBUTOR

REVIEW-COPY
JOHN BENJAMINS B.V.
Publisher
Amsteldijk 44
P.O.Box 52519
1007 HA AMSTERDAM
The Netherlands

JOHN BENJAMINS PUBLISHING COMPANY
AMSTERDAM/PHILADELPHIA

1983

"La littérature représente le monde comme une question, jamais en définitive comme une réponse."

Roland Barthes

"Admettons que la littérature commence au moment où la littérature devient question. Une fois la page écrite, est présente dans cette page la question qui, peut-être à son insu, n'a cessé d'interroger l'écrivain tandis qu'il écrivait."

Maurice Blanchot

"L'objet d'un vrai critique devrait être de découvrir quel problème l'auteur, sans le savoir ou le sachant, s'est posé et de chercher s'il l'a résolu ou non."

Paul Valéry

TABLE OF CONTENTS

ACKNOWLEDGMENTS

My very special thanks go to Charles Barker for the marvelous editing he has done. If this book can give the impression of being written in English, this is due to him.

Part of this book has already appeared in *Philosophica*, I wish to thank the editors of this journal, Leo Apostel and Dirk Batens, for their kind permission to use and modify these materials.

I would also like to express my gratitude to Renée Vanwinkel for her competence and patience in typing the manuscript in its several versions, as well as to Suzanne Roos for complementary revisions of the text.

Brussels 1981—Yale 1982.

0. INTRODUCTION

How does language work and how does it affect literariness? Traditionally, literary criticism, not to mention general theories of literature, has not specifically dealt with these questions, which it deemed of little relevance. Language is used mostly to communicate and inform. Works of art, however, even when they are discursive, cannot be characterized on such grounds. What seems, instead, to mark literary discourse most distinctively is its capacity to become *autonomous*. The autonomy of forms with respect to historical boundaries can only reinforce the critic to uphold the claim that literary works can and should be studied in themselves because they stand by themselves.

Literary discourse nonetheless pertains to the wider realm of language. Hence the basic question that we should raise is: How should we conceive language such as to render literature and its relative autonomy possible? This question implies, in its very formulation, that we cannot take this autonomy as a starting point; neither can we take for granted literature as a *sui generis* mode of discourse.

Our question is a philosophical question in the sense that it necessitates the development of a general view of language and understanding that accounts, among other things, for style and *poiesis*. As a framework for language as a whole, this view is meant to relate general notions with one another, and particular concepts, such as irony, repression, metaphor, or indeterminacy will not be mentioned independently of these more general principles they are supposed to instantiate.

Our treatment of the question raised above will exceed the traditional requirements and possibilities of linguistic analysis, which excludes figurative language, and rhetoric in general, as an object of its theoretical ambitions. As we know, its questions are different from the one which we raise here. A philosophical view of language offers a different perspective by using different concepts, more adequate to answer the questions it addresses.

How shall we proceed to arrive at our basic concepts? The very idea of a philosophical view already suggests the answer. The question of the possibility of language and of its literariness cannot be comprehended in terms of preconceived categories or theories; if it were, the question raised would be begged instead of being explicitly asked as a question. The question is here the essential notion to be taken into account and the answer must then count questions, hence answers, as the grounding notion in the theory to be constructed. This, and nothing else, renders the question and its answer philosophical. Philosophy handles general problems and does not take any answer for granted: it starts from the questions themselves, whatever its other presuppositions which cannot be dispensed with. A philosophical view of language must then provide an answer as to how we can confront problems as such in language and distinguish them from their solutions. By offering an answer, a philosophical conception of language must necessarily confront the problem of answering which, as a problem, refers back to the question of questioning. Language, like the other human activities or instruments, enables us to deal with our problems, i.e. to express them, or their solution if it is possible. This is the reason why a philo-sophical theory of language must be rooted in the question-answer complex. This, quite evidently, could be denied and some other conception be preferred. But such a view would provide an answer without having inquired into ques-tioning and would have thereby answered the question of questioning without having ever stipulated that it would, i.e. without having really *asked* it at all. Such a theory could nonetheless be valid, as a partial view, but it could not pretend to have addressed the question raised at the outset, which requires a general conception of language and from which, consequently, nothing can be left out or presupposed. This question, then, cannot remain itself out of the picture since, as a question, it defines the basic requirements of the picture. The answer must specify how language can handle non-linguistic questions (as well as linguistic ones) linguistically and nonetheless take them up *as questions*, i.e. as being identical in a way that transcends their diversity of origin and resolu-tion. This way is language.

The approach developed in the following pages is new in more than one respect. It offers a unified theory of language and meaning based on questioning. This question view has undoubtedly been anticipated by several authors, though it has never before been fully and systematically articulated as it is here. We have, therefore, coined a new term for this philosophical view: *problematology*. However, the question of questioning will be restricted here to its impact on language and literature.

The need to unify our view of language can be illustrated by the still pre-vailing gap between sentence and text. To specify the meaning of a sentence is to state another sentence, as we know from everyday experience. How should we answer if asked to express the meaning of a book? Should we rewrite it in a different form for the person who questions us? If we commit ourselves to some sentential semantics, as it has been done since the time of the Greeks, we inevitably fall on such a paradox. Strikingly enough, this gap between sentence and text has never been seriously challenged. Philosophers in the Anglo-American tradition have followed sentential semantics as it has been immortalized by Frege. Literary critics, who nonetheless reject such a narrow view of language, have not endeavored to provide another one, better suited for the purpose of textual analysis. In fact, we may ask ourselves whether the conception according to which each text is an encoded version or interpretation of some other text does not allow for a displacement of the substitution view at the level of textuality by relying on the idea of repetition. The question deserves to be asked, but literary critics very seldom inquire into the philosophical foundations of their practice, mostly because they are studying particular texts or authors. As to general theories of literature, they proceed from the idea that the autonomy of literary works implies theoretical autonomy at the reflexive level as well. When they do not, they merely equate their endeavors with the new philosophy of language as it should emerge from their rejection of any sort of analytic philosophy, thereby following Heidegger in this respect.

Nevertheless, we should *ask* the question we are dealing with. We cannot assume that this is the correct way of conceiving language and that these theories have the answer without having raised the question as such. We can even suspect that theories which model themselves upon sentences exclusively, or texts exclusively, are equally wrong. We must then ask the question of the unity of language without presupposing that there is an unbridgeable gap between sentence and text, without taking for granted that sentential semantics or any other semantics is *a priori* the ultimate model of meaning. Problematology can, I think, bring a conclusive solution to such problems. In earlier publications, I have already suggested that questioning is not only the essential feature of science, where it takes place in a specific way, but also that language in all its generality can be conceptualized in terms of questioning. The basic reason for this lies in the fact that we always have a question in mind when we speak or write. What is in question is usually called the topic or meaning. Language use is not an inquiry in the same sense as science is an inquiry, but it nonetheless involves the resolution of a question. When we ask ourselves what a sentence or a text means, we obviously raise a question. But when we produce this very same sentence or this very same text, we also deal with a question, though we do not say "This is the question asked." We just answer it. The question we are dealing with is simply repressed into the answer which expresses what was in question as being now out-of-the question. This difference gives rise to a judgment. What was problematic is affirmed as non-problematic. The answer represses its own status as an answer by not referring explicitly to the question it answers. What it expresses is something else: the question to which it corresponds. The answer does not refer to itself but to something else. Logicians call this fact referentiality or, more simply, reference. They fail to see this as a dynamic phenomenon and restrict themselves to the componential and static analysis of referential items, without investigating what makes it possible. Referentiality is just the logico-grammatical aspect of the process of expression of answers – or, in other words, of repression of the questionable into the assertoric. Statements are answers. What they state is not stipulated as such; they only state it. From a syntactic point of view, there is a deleting of interrogatives which takes place for each term and renders it unquestionable as it appears in the statement. Speaking or writing is thinking: there is a passage from a question toward an answer in the production of any discourse. The answer can be one term, one sentence, or a whole text. In each case, a question which was there, so to speak, vanishes into some referential item *corresponding* to what was in question and suppressing it. The subject-predicate structure is only one way for the human mind to relate the unproblematic to what was problematic before. The *presence* of the subject as *substance* is to be seen as the answer corresponding to something which is (at present) what it was not (before). Questions and answers are the units of thought, not statements or signs. Semiotics, too, failed to see why a sign refers to (stands for) something other than itself and how this is a dynamic process. This is a consequence of the presence of some question-answer complex which is not found only in language. A road sign, for instance, it at the same time a problem and a solution: it is meant to establish a difference in our behavior and to suggest specific new answers as well as new questions related to the use of this sign.

It is not necessary to outline the content of the chapters of this volume in this *Introduction*, but a short description of the book may be helpful to indicate how problematology can contribute to the theory of literature.

The unification of sentential and textual semantics is more than a goal and is not just a presupposition. It gives access to the unity of language and is achieved by showing that we always relate *what* is said or *what* is written to the question that this 'what' expresses and which designates an answered question. In the case of sentences, the relationship between a single statement and the question it answers is established through interrogative clauses. An interrogative clause is a relative proposition, introduced by an interrogative pronoun, that characterizes some term. The interrogative stands for this term. By an essential characterization, we mean, along with the *Port-Royal* grammar, that the term *in question* in the interrogative expansion cannot be suppressed without altering the meaning of the subsequent text. Most of the time, terms are used in every-day speech without such clauses, whereby the addressee, reader, or interlocutor assumes that the question of what they mean and refer to is settled. Speaking is thinking in the sense that the questions raised by the terms we use in speech are solved, proving, thereby, that we do not need to refer to what they stand for by making clear which interrogatives they correspond to. These interrogatives and the relative clauses in turn refer back to the questions which have arisen about them in the mind of the speaker and which he wants to specify as being solved the way he says they are. In the case of whole texts, *what* is said or written should be taken as a unit of language and should also be related to its cor-responding question(s). What exactly does this 'what' above cover? The ques-tion(s) referred to is (are) what is not literally expressed by the text. Each sen-tence of a given text literally deals with a given question, but the text as a whole cannot be understood by adding these questions one after the other. The text as a whole refers in a non-literal way to a problematic for which it provides (an) answer(s). If the problem that a given text answers is known from the text's socio-historical context or from an explicit stipulation of the problem in that text, no rhetorical procedure is necessary to convey textual meaning, i.e. the question dealt with by the text, which cannot be posed literally. The non-literal meaning of the text *qua* text (its textuality) resolves itself most of the time into a literal one in everyday language usage.

Literary texts, on the other hand, are characterized by their autonomization from the problems they treat, leading to a rhetoricalization of these problems to which no literal ready-made substitute can correspond. Ideology is the cause of such treatment. An ideology must be able to answer all questions with which it is confronted. This is clearly impossible. The questions it must deal with are treated as rhetorical with respect to the available or derivable 'answers' of the ideology in question. This, in turn, implies that one needs a *medium* (or media-tor) that transforms a non-rhetorical or real question into a rhetorical one. The expression of the rhetorical problem can then have a literal counterpart in the ideology. This process of mediatization is called *fiction.* Questions challenging a thought system are therefore fictionalized: they are dealt with as if they were what they are not, whereby illusion is created. If questions were not treated this way, the ideological system could be called into question from the inside and be literally challenged on its own terms. The ideological system would not remain closed in upon itself. Fiction takes up questions confronting the ideology and rhetoricalizes them via another but derived problematic issue that is solved in a literary text and that argumentatively suggests an *a priori* ideological 'answer' to the original question challenging the ideology.

Literature displaces ideological problems, or *ideas* if we prefer this word, and thereby acquires autonomy with respect to them. It institutes a new relationship with reality. Literature auto-contextualizes the problems that it creates, i.e., it gives them a specific form with respect to everyday language for which problems are totally external and, so to speak, 'realistic'. This auto-contextualization is *poiesis*. The basic law ruling the poetic process is a consequence of the problematological difference, according to which questions (or problems) and answers (or solutions) are always marked off in some way or other, e.g. by form. When this difference applies to fiction, we call it the *law of symbolic weakening*. The more explicit a problem is, the less figurative the language used to deal with it and vice versa. In other terms, symbolic language and rhetorical devices are used more in a text when the text itself does not distinctively stipulate what is problematic and what is not. The minimal level of rhetoricity, so to speak, is defined by the textual ordering which is by itself a non-literal answer to the question raised by reading literal statements in succession.

'What does it mean?' is then a question intrinsic to literary texts as a result of the fictionalization of the problematological difference between questions and answers through figurative language or specific textual arrangements which may be themselves posing a question to the reader by their unusual structure. Ordinary discourse refers to a context where problems are defined or understood in terms of an external situation. Fiction, through an act of *poiesis*, creates this environment that would not have existed otherwise. The question of the questions referred to in fiction arises, hence the need for an interpretation. When these questions are specified, such a need is narrowed down to a progressive reading of the text which is sufficient to enable the reader to grasp the resolution of the questions, as in detective stories.

Interpretation always consists in relating the text as answer to the questions it answers, i.e. in grasping its status as an answer. This status as an answer is often implicit and literal, i.e. immanent to the answer, so that, as a corollary, understanding is mental and goes without saying. When it is not literal, it is contextual, in which case understanding is implicit too.

Texts answer questions which are rooted in a socio-historical context. What is the relationship between the corresponding answers? The expressive sublimation of these questions into literary answers ensures the autonomization of the latter. Answers are autonomous, but not in the same sense as literature is. What is common, however, is that answers, whatever they are, result from the repression of their status as answers. That status, in turn, renders meaning an implicit feature of discourse. Literary answers are historically autonomous and this constitutes the very historicity of literature. There is no other way of conceiving the historicity of literary discourse than to see it in terms of auto-contextualized derived ideas. These ideas are ideologically derived: they neither reflect the historical infrastructure, nor represent a totally independent series of ideas that could be studied as a succession of literary genres or independent, cross-cultural codes. The first impossibility possibilitates autonomy, the second, relativity and change.

The interpretation of literary texts consists first of all in reading the questions embodied in them. This gives rise to literal readings which must be put together because the text from which they derive is a whole. The questions dealt with in each constituent answer of a text refer to a unified problematic: each answer is in reality a guiding principle for discovering a non-literal answer associated with the text as a whole, i.e. with textuality. The questions raised by literary texts are formalized. They are not literally expressed, and literal readings only limit the range of possible non-literal anwers to the question of interpretation. What remains problematic, inherent in the very nature of literary textuality, is what does not lend itself to a literal reformulation; no substitutive translation of the text could render it totally transparent in all its meanings or readings. Texts, literary or not, admit several readings, among which a non-literal one is always (and *a priori*) possible. Texts do not say what they mean even when they express what they answer. They express it without saying it and this leaves room, even at the level of minimal rhetoric, for multiple readings, though we must recognize that, when the problem is clearly stipulated, various meanings are factored out. Nevertheless, nothing will prove that the real questions are the avowed ones.

What renders literary interpretation more complicated is fiction's intrinsic feature: auto-contextualization. This implies relative historical autonomy but also the absolute necessity of finding out the problems dealt with, and hence the meaning in literature, which are not readily at hand and which always resist a literal expression that would exhaust the content of fiction. The literal readings are the limits of a consistent interpretation but no substitute for it.

Interpretation is then a questioning process implied by literary texts. It corresponds to the questioning embedded in these texts. What is constantly evolving, because it is not limited to what is literally to be found in the texts themselves, is the questioning process to which they give rise. Texts survive the questions they were meant to solve by means of the questions addressed to them throughout history.

This view of interpretation may sound similar to hermeneutics and its literary version called 'reception theory'. In fact, *poiesis* cannot be restricted to the sole problematic of meaning. These theories, though touching on the question of questioning, do not provide philosophical foundations for their undertakings in opposition to alternative views, which remain equally plausible. We do not find that there is any theory of language that could validate their claim (which would present itself as a mere standpoint, alongside other competing ones) according to which meaning is reading or interpreting is questioning. There is no systematic analysis of language or questioning in these doctrines, however helpful they may appear when the gap has to be filled.

All this will be substantiated further in this book, which is meant to be a study of literary discourse as it can emerge from a more general framework that purports to integrate discourse as a whole. Some ideas will sound familiar to literary critics, and my hope is that this book will thereby strengthen the credibility of problematology, to which the following pages intend to serve as an introduction for the English speaking reader. My second wish is for philosophers to see in this book an incentive to look upon literature and literary theory as a source of inspiration and as an opportunity for justifying general claims about thinking and judging.

1. THE CLASSICAL CONCEPTION OF MEANING
AND ITS SHORTCOMINGS

1.1. *Meaning in a literary setting*

The prestige of literary theory in philosophical circles has increased considerably in recent years due to the philosophers' search for a generalized conception of meaning. The necessity of leaving aside once and for all the traditional theories of signification modeled upon isolated sentences or statements can be illustrated by the following question: If to know the meaning of a sentence is to be capable of producing another sentence, are we ready to say that the understanding of any book, let alone a literary text, means being able to rewrite it?

This is where propositional theory breaks down. We will make its content more precise later, but we can see immediately that a theory which rests upon the simple idea that the comprehension and the study of any piece of language, from a word to a text, should begin and end with the proposition can hardly be systematized into an overall conception of understanding, although this has been attempted by many philosophers, logicians, and linguists. They proceed as if an adequate view of language as a whole, as it is actually spoken and written, could be given by using *ad hoc* sentences, taken out of any context as examples for subsequent generalization. As a result, those sentences are usually presented disconnected from any speech continuum, i.e. in a 'de-contextualized' way. They are as unlikely to be actually used as the famous *The present King of France is bald.* Nobody but philosophers could ever have uttered such a sentence. When propositions are presented as being related to one another, it is in order to exhibit strictly formal and *a priori* links, exemplifying more often than not philosophical quibbles that language users seldom encounter in real life. After all, who cares about the present King of France, or about the fact that, if one ever mentioned him, one would use a name or a vacuous description? Fastidious as it may appear, it may be beneficial to recall some of the most famous examples and analyses put forth in the numerous volumes written on this topic and to realize how narrowly meaning has been conceived by those who claimed to explain meaning within the *general* framework of language use as a *general* phenomenon inherent in the very nature of language and, for the most audacious, of symbolism, and consequently, of culture.

In fact, these writers never seem to have perceived the damaging consequences of their theory. But someone else did it for them. No wonder that the man in question proved to be a master in storytelling, one of the greatest: Jorge Luis Borges.

In "Pierre Ménard, author of the *Quixote*", Borges introduces us to a character who has decided to devote himself to the rewriting of Cervantes' masterpiece. Precisely because it is impossible to render Cervantes' book by one substitutional, epitomizing statement, i.e. by one tautology, the interpreter has to crystallize the *Quixote* into another version that would be as perfect as a tautology in its mission of rendering meaning term by term, but would be more global. If some global substitution could be offered, it could not but be the perfect interpretation of the work. Hence, in order to grasp the intrinsic message of the *Quixote*, Ménard sees no other course than to rewrite it entirely, committing himself in the most absurd manner to the substitution view of meaning which is what the semantics of the propositional theory of language is about. What can be more quixotic than literally reproducing the *Quixote*? Pierre Ménard appears here as *Don Xerox*. His project is senseless, but Ménard pursues it to its logical conclusion with the consistency of the propositional theorist. Once we – the readers – accept his method, Ménard looks as reasonable as many logicians or philosophers of language. Like someone who is determined to write down the mental product of his own understanding, Ménard sets himself the task of duplicating with the utmost perfection the text he is obsessed with. His faithfulness to the text requires that its reproduction be unaltered even in its most minute details. Is not the perfect substitutional version of a text, as of any piece of language, its *identical* reproduction? "Cervantes' text and Ménard's are verbally identical, but the second is almost infinitely richer" (Borges 1970: 69) as literary project[1] and as a literary work of art.[2]

Are philosophers interested in meaning compelled to become Pierre Ménard's of some sort when they endeavor to understand understanding texts instead of sentences?

1.2. *The arguments for the defense*

We shall not neglect those arguments in the course of this study. One argument that presents itself immediately is the following: perhaps we should acknowledge some kind of distinction between at least two varieties of meaning on the basis of the units of language taken into consideration: sentence *versus* discourse. Different rules would apply to each one of these entities. Or should we rather seek the difference in the well-established distinction of literature and ordinary language: fiction *versus* referential in the discourse? Or should we perhaps focus on the modality of their expression: spoken *versus* written language?

These objections beg the question: they all presuppose the validity of the propositional theory of language, which they try to preserve, despite its obvious inability to bridge the gap from sentence to text. But why should we accept all those lacunae, which seem to be invoked only to perpetuate the myth of the incommensurability of divergent levels of meaning? This, of course, does not imply that there is no difference between fiction and non-fiction, for instance. Our point is simply that those distinctions should not serve as a pretext to ratify a preestablished view of meaning which does not apply as a general conception, in spite of its claim to do so. The fact that fiction differs from non-ficton does not prove that this is due to the nature of meaning, nor does it imply that one should relegate fiction to a *sui generis* realm of signification.

But why *should* we believe in the fragmentation of understanding? Why would the nature of meaning change according to the length or the modality of linguistic expressions? Is not meaning inherent in language, spoken or written, fictional or veridical? Worse: why should we go along with the view that *there is no unity of language* in its various manifestations?

1.3. *More about the propositional theory of language and its semantic consequences: the Xerox theory of meaning*

The substitution view of meaning, or *Xerox-semantics*, derives directly from the propositional theory of language. We can summarize this theory's major points as follows: language should and can be adequately studied by focusing on isolated sentences, statements, or individual propositions. They independently reveal their own logical structure and even their own meaning and they do not need, therefore, to be inserted within any context of utterance, or in the natural environment of their production, implicit (presuppositions) or explicit, subjective or social. They bear alone all the information that language users need to know in order to understand them.[3] If we call a *proposition* the meaning of such sentences, we must say that, by declaring their meaning through what they affirm or deny, such sentences also give their meaning, that is, the proposition which expresses their sense. Just as *John is tall* means that 'John is tall', the proposition is another sentence which is substitutable for the original one to the extent of being semantically identical with it. The basis for such a substitutability needs only to be logical. But what do we mean exactly by *logical*?

A century ago, Frege gave a systematic answer, corresponding to a generalized view of language as a whole. But, quite obviously, the propositional theory *as an idea* and as an effective principle of linguistic analysis existed long before that. It is in fact a legacy from the Greeks. One of its consequences is the priority given to written language over spoken language, since what is written must (at least *in principle*) encompass all the elements necessary to its understanding, without requiring anything else. We also find in the propositional theory an explanation of the close association which has so often prevailed between (propositional) logic and grammar (cf. Lyons 1968: 8-10, 16-18), between the laws of thought and the ways of expressing it:

> "the definition of the major grammatical classes in Greek thought, 'nouns' and 'verbs', was made on logical grounds: i.e. as constituents of a proposition." (Lyons 1968:11)

Written language has something in common with declarative sentences or propositions: it should be capable, due to its inner structure, of furnishing all the elements necessary to its understanding, although it does not always do this effectively. Appeal to context is often an imperative, but language must at least possess the structures that render such a self-sufficiency possible. If we always had to seek the meaning of what is said beyond what is said, what would be the point of saying it? Sometimes we have to do so, but it is not true that everything which is said or written should be understood figuratively. Literal meaning exists. The *isolated sentence* which precisely embodies *all* the information needed is the *proposition*. That is why the proposition has always served as a model to linguists, philosophers, and logicians. It possesses the virtue of perfection, namely semantic autonomy; it declares its meaning, it even says *what* it means. This denoting whatness is, in fact, the basis of the *classical reference theory*, which is the systematized substitution view of meaning that Frege gave us.

Where do we find those neat sentences, those statements which, by being self-sufficient, offer all the elements analysis should lay bare? In mathematics, where language occurs in its purest form, the ambiguity so often present in natural language has disappeared. Propositions, there, display their naked signification, and by looking closely at the composition of a mathematical proposition, we can gain a sure insight into the way language functions in general.

Natural language, according to propositional theorists, also possesses the inner structure of mathematical language, but in less explicit form. Ordinary language is, by nature, ambiguous, and its structures are less apparent. Nonetheless, the result of any language use must eventually be the same: understanding. How can we understand any phrase at all if we are not capable of ascribing one meaning to it, i.e. of resolving its ambiguity when it is ambiguous? The same process which is at work in the formal language of mathematics must manifest itself in ordinary language, albeit below the surface. As a result, ordinary language can be formalized, like mathematics, and what will emerge out of its logicization are the univocal meanings, the propositions, that language-receivers always decode in fact. Formalization reveals *one* meaning and helps to discover it.

Frege also wished to build up an ideography, a perfect symbolic language, to eradicate ambiguities of expression in mathematics, where they proved costly due to the paradoxes they generated. His basic question was to show how a sentence *could* convey its own intelligibility. Statements do this naturally in mathematics, or they should if the symbolism and the rules are adequate. A sentence does this, but by other means, in ordinary language, where logical form is an underlying structure that expresses what is univocally meant in language that could otherwise give rise to several readings. Being the result of a less rule-oriented procedure (that is, of understanding, in which Frege had no interest), this logical phrase gives nonetheless *the* meaning of the understood sentence, as it does for all possible sentences since it is in the very nature of language to convey the means of its own understandability.

Perhaps a more fundamental question to be solved is why we have propositions at all, i.e. why the proposition constitutes the most basic unit of thought. We know why; we should rather ask *how* language achieves its semantic perfection in propositions. What makes a proposition a proposition?

Two aspects of Frege's analysis are of interest to us here: the reformulation or renewal of the propositional theory, and the classical reference theory which is his theory of meaning, his reformulation of the substitution view. To put it in a nutshell, these two aspects constitute a theory of terms (and of their complementarity) and a theory of propositions. Both are, of course, interrelated. Let us begin with the classical reference theory (of meaning). I call it *classical*, in contrast to another version of referentiality which will be given in the next chapter along with Frege's theory of terms, and which does not concern us at present since we are here exclusively interested in meaning.

Terms and propositions have both *sense* and *reference*: they express (sense) something (reference). When some definite sense and some definite reference are correlated, one precise signification is the result. This holds for names as well as for predicates and sentences: the signification of a sentence depends on the signification of the name and the predicate composing it. This is Frege's *principle of composition.* Two sentences have the same signification when, although they are expressed differently (two senses), they say the same thing (one reference). *What* the first says is declared by the second, and vice versa. They both say the same thing; this *denoting whatness* renders them substitutable for each other. They declare a common proposition, i.e. *what* they say. Their reference is an identical truth, despite the two differing expressions by means of which they declare it.

What is significant in the account just given is that it establishes the fundamental tenet of the propositional theory of meaning: the meaning of a sentence is a substitutable statement, which says the same thing, that is, *refers* to the same thing — a truth-value (Frege), or a fact (Wittgenstein) — by expressing it differently. *What* the sentences say is identical, but the duplication adds something by explicating in a different way *what* is being referred to. To the principle of composition, one should add a principle of extension that stipulates how the components should be analyzed.

In spite of its general credibility, Frege's view as such has given rise to many difficulties, due to its propositionalist outlook.

(a) Not all the sentences we use are declarative; many of them do not declare anything, but ask, evoke, request, and so forth. Do they have no meaning for the simple reason that they have no truth-value to which they refer, as they would if they declared *something*? Even if we assimilated the meaning of these so-called illocutionary acts to their propositional content, we would lose something along the way, namely the specificity of their original form, and the illocutionary force meant in their employment, which would disappear in the propositional translation.

(b) The meaning of a sentence is a proposition which affirms the same, and in so doing, preserves the truth-value of what the first sentence affirms. The relation of sameness implies not only possible substitution, but, most importantly, the existence of one identical reference (truth-value) corresponding to two expressions. As far as propositions are concerned, they result in a single signification, identical for both sentences. Then, *John is tall* means 'Grass is green', since, although the two sentences express different thoughts, they refer to the same truth-value, i.e. the True. All possible objections against our own criticisms could but presuppose what is to be explained, namely the semantic affinity between the two thoughts, or their relationship to *one* Truth-value (which, then, is not solely true but has something more, namely a semantic content that establishes the affinity of the two thoughts to the extent of rendering them substitutable).

(c) Frege, of course, realized all this. That is why he laid down his principle of composition. When judgments are considered as autonomous pieces of language, one's only recourse is to consider the elements they contain. Frege agrees with the basic requirement of the propositional theory, but wants to apply it in his own terms. Sense, *Sinn*, and reference, *Bedeutung*, are what must be carefully singled out in the compositional analysis of the sentence. In the above example, *John* refers to some entity which is not the entity referred to by the name *Grass*, and hence sentences in which these words occur cannot carry identical meanings. The case of fiction, adds Frege, is an exception, for non-literal meanings occur there due — as he would say — to the non-referential use of terms. Two judgments involving them, therefore, cannot be substituted for one another.

Let us provisionally accept this principle. It commits us nevertheless to un-wanted consequences, in addition to those of its exclusive dependence on the components of a statement to derive its meaning, even when sentences are compared as independent wholes. First, in spite of what Frege himself said, names seem to receive a signification (sense + reference) by themselves, quite inde-pendently of the sentences wherein they *have* to occur *to have* this meaning. Second, vacuous names denote the same reality, i.e. nothing, and express this, albeit differently. The result is the same truth-value: the False. That makes them substitutable, equi-referential, according to Frege's definition of identity. *Meursault killed an Arab* has then the same meaning as *Roquentin killed an Arab*, though one does not find the latter formulation in Camus's *L'Etranger*. One possible objection against the latter objection would be as follows: the ob-jection is not valid because Frege's view of names does not apply to fiction, where they are evidently vacuous. Outside fiction, by definition of the word *fiction*, they are meant to be used denotatively, and as a result, names which do not refer to anything are not names. In the Fregean framework, however, names can be deprived of reference and still have a *sense*. But Russell has quite rightly objected that, whenever we want to supply the meaning of a whole sentence, we cannot but resort to the analysis of its components, i.e. the names composing both statements, the meaning, and the meaningful proposition must contain names with the same reference in order for the judgments to be semantically substitutable. Otherwise, *John is tall* could also mean 'The grass is green'. But, if this must be the case, then obviously, names must *always* be considered as referential, as being the referring items *par excellence*, and consequently, the principle of composition must imply the use of the principle of extensionality. Names must have a reference, if those principles are to characterize an analysis of meaning as a substitutable proposition. As to empty names, Russell will later say that they are truncated descriptions, empty predicates, and that, logically speaking, they cannot be considered as subjects of sentences. We can reply that names are often used in language without any denoting purpose even when they refer to some existing being. In other terms, we do use words without intending to say that something correspond to them in the real world, and it does not even matter whether such a correspondence prevails or not. We do not look into the real world to see *whether* something corresponds to our terms and *what* really corresponds to them. We are then capable of understanding a sentence such as *Napoleon lost at Waterloo*, without going outside our room and without traveling into the past. To understand language, we do not have to look outside language and decompose everything we hear or read until we arrive at its un-analyzable elements. Fiction, as we shall see later, rests upon the fact that names are often used referentially. How could fiction otherwise give the illusion of representing reality? The Fregean argument of recourse to fiction does not hold: it amounts to saying that a name denotes something, except when it does not. Does it prove that names always refer, unless they are used fictionally? Does it imply that intrinsically names are referential, because it is their purpose to be so, when we know that fictional contexts present names without reference? In short, names must have a reference because they must and when they do not, they are fictive names in spite of their appearance as names. Frege's argument cannot be retained, for, it begs the question, *ex hypothesi* fiction is defined by the lack of reference. The consequence of all this is that the principle of composition is inadequate to account for meaning in literature.

> "Nowhere in current theory of literature is it clearer than in the dispute over the problem of definition that the reference theory of meaning is the barrier to progress; it is still the basis of all thought on the subject." (Ellis 1974: 26)

Frege's views have so much dominated the analysis of language that sub-sequent studies of that topic have adopted if not his conclusions, at least his methodological standpoint of compositionality. Unless, of course, we recognize that this standpoint had been accepted *a priori*, and that all systematization Frege based on it had the sole effect of increasing the adherence to it. Worse, even literary criticism has established the demarcation line between fiction and veridical discourse in terms of referentiality: fictional language would be defined as the non-referential discourse *par excellence.*

Our claim is that Frege's view, which, in order to hold at all, must presuppose the principle of composition, renders textual analysis impossible precisely because it is analytical. Sentences, when combined to form a continuous discourse, display their intelligibility by the (logical) connections existing between the respective components of each sentence. The meaning of a text is then an aggregation of isolated meanings, and not a unity which is meaningful *per se* in its very continuity. But what would render the $n + 1$th sentence, in a Fregean textual combination, necessary to the understanding of the whole, i.e. the n preceding phrases, which are allegedly understandable by themselves? If we are consistent, we ought to say that whole chapters of books could logically be disposed of, without causing any loss to the understanding of the preceding ones. But this *aprogressive* view of meaning would not even work for analytically built up books like Proust's *A la recherche du temps perdu*, Joyce's *Ulysses,* or Musil's *Mann ohne Eigenschaften.* And we can affirm beyond dispute that it *could not* work with more conventional novels such as detective stories, and more generally with all those where the beginning requires an end to make sense at all.

Frege sees the intelligibility of sentences as a truth-functional notion: the meaning of a set of sentences is reducible to the meaning of its composing sentences, just as in mathematics, or just as the meaning of a sentence is reducible to the meaning of its composing terms (name and predicate). It is a logical relationship. The combination of sentences is a logical one, and can be characterized accordingly as truth-functional, i.e. as a function of elementary truth-values.

Notice that the process just described has nothing to do with fiction or literature but applies to texts and speech continua in general. Meaning is aggregative, in the sense that two sentences can be studied through the now classical theory of connectives, as it can be found in all the textbooks of elementary logic. What is true for a compound made up from two sentences logically applies to longer compounds.

Let us finally mention a strange argument put forth against the propositional theory, but which, in my eyes, rather confirms it, or at any rate does not alter it substantially.

As we have seen, the credibility of the propositional theory derives mainly from the fact that, in given circumstances, a sentence can convey all the information necessary to its understanding, and that, in such a case, appeal to the context of utterance or appearance adds nothing which would modify the compositional knowledge. When comparing a sentence to its corresponding proposition, we see that the former affirms *what* the latter says, and that both affirm literally the same thing. Linguistically, they may be indistinguishable.[4] This is the case with declarative sentences since the meaning of a sentence, i.e. a proposition, is itself declarative. That is why one often sees the word *sentence* employed for *proposition*, and vice versa.

Being indistinguishable from one another, at least in their linguistic aspect, propositions are the sole entities that can be scientifically *observed* and which present themselves as nothing but declarative sentences. They have been said to be useless and unobservable, as far as their linguistic specificity is concerned. *John is tall* means 'John is tall': we here face the same sentence and some authors, following Quine, have refused to call the former a sentence and the latter a proposition, since obviously the same *sentence* is uttered. Occam's razor commands the eradication of the entity called proposition from our theoretical language: if a proposition which stipulates the meaning of a sentence does not declare the same sentence, it cannot be its meaning; if it is different, how can it be its meaning?

In fact, this distinction between sentences and propositions can only prevail in a theoretical world where propositions would cease to be linguistic, i.e. sentential items. We always fall back on sentences when some meaning is *given*. But the ground for such a differentiation lies elsewhere. Propositions are neither mental nor metaphysical entities of any kind; they are simply introduced to characterize a world where sentences can say something else than what they declare, if they declare at all. This reality leaves room for the gap between literal and figurative meaning, and enables us to conceive of a linguistic world where all sentences suggest, evoke, imply (in a non-logical sense), request to think or act, and so on. Such a world is of no interest to the logician. And when he takes a look at it, it is with the secret hope or the avowed theoretical claim that natural language will normally abide by the context-free rules of logic. This he calls, quite appropriately, in the light of the military connotation of the word: *regimentation*.

Even when logicians, linguists, or philosophers count propositions as superfluous entities, they still hold on to the propositional theory. Their criticism only applies to a model of language where declarative sentences are cast in the leading role. The basic question is to know whether we can continue to hold on to such a theory.

1.4. *Context matters*

What are the general reservations to be made about logicism and more generally the propositional theory and the classical reference conception of meaning ensuing from it?

(a) Sentences, in normal circumstances, are not isolated. They occur within definite contexts of utterance; this is not any more incidental to the analysis of language, than it is to its employment. And, in speaking of context, I have something precise in mind, something that conforms to everyday notions and effective usage. I refuse to take that notion, as many a logician does, as a rag bag of confused ideas or a contraption invoked *ad hoc* to make up for the already existing, and failing, explanatory devices of actual use. Context is a relationship between language users and their relevant background knowledge: it is defined by a speaker, *I;* by an addressee, *you, him,* or *her*; *and* by the knowledge they share *and* ascribe to one another. Context is then a determining factor in the pursuit of any dialogue. From the social point of view, each use of language is the continuation of a previous one: language is socially speaking through us as if there had never been any break is the conversation. A new dialogue is always socially old and sometimes so much so that it sounds wholly conventional.

(b) Sentences are never separable from the preceding ones uttered in the context of the initial production. When only one sentence is uttered, it is nonetheless situated within a context where other sentences have been uttered and with respect to which that sentence is produced, as in dialogues.

All this renders rather vain the traditional endeavors to pursue meaning, truth, reference, or simply empirical bearing in the sentence itself, as if structurally it *had* to possess all those properties. However, the conditions of actual use enable us to get the information about the sentence from outside so that it does not *have* to bear the whole weight of the knowledge to be communicated. Here I shall permit myself to be more of an empiricist than those who profess, by tradition, to be so. Why should we decide *in abstracto*, i.e. quite unnaturally, whether a name is vacuous or referential, whether an expression is attributive or not, e.g. whether *The Present King of France is bald* is meaningless or false? In fact, we are bound to attribute some relevance to such queries *if* we take sentences as independent wholes: then, *they* must bear the load of referentiality, empiricalness, and so on. But if we are ready to concede the fact that habitual sentences, unlike the Russellian examples, are written and spoken within given contexts, then all the dilemmas of Frege and Russell vanish. Considered abstractly, it may be the case that a name means different objects, but in real life we also know to whom or to what a sentence really refers. Do names, then, still have to have a denoting function, and, if not, do they have to be called something else than names in virtue of an *a priori* conception of language and empiricalness? Is it not unempirical to ascribe to language all the empirical requirements of our relationship to the world, *while the very fact that we resort to language reveals that it is a mode of actualization of that relationship*? In fact, the latter is ensured not semantically, as logicists claimed, but pragmatically. I repeat my question: who, and in what situation, would speak of the Present King of France *and* who would do it in a philosophically problematic way? The empiricist deconstruction of language leads to an empirically illegitimate reconstruction based on what language should be and not on what it actually is, except perhaps in mathematics.

To put my conclusion in a nutshell: isolated sentences do not exist, and the idea that we can single one out from its context of usage is a fallacy, which, of course, does not mean that, in a given context, we cannot isolate a sentence from the speech sequence in which it originally occurred. This 'isolation' amounts to the insertion of the sentence into a new context, rather than to a decontextualization. Besides, this reinsertion cannot serve as a basis for a theoretical standpoint on language in general since this is only a particular *use* of language.

(c) As a consequence, isolated sentences, i.e. 'decontextualized' expressions, can be considered as abstractions, and not as models for the study of our real employment of language. We do not speak or write *in abstracto*. Not even in science are expressions employed totally context-free. Understanding is not limited to the capacity of recognizing that expressions are true. Context in science plays a minimal role. Science is by itself a definite context of utterance: the context in which all references to context are to be eradicated as much as possible. The important point here is that the procedures followed in science are the opposite of those adopted by everyday language users. Natural language is only possible on the basis of contextual information. In contrast to science, one always addresses oneself to somebody in particular to tell him things which would be of no interest for someone else and which may even be false or quite ambiguous to everybody else. One cannot, and does not have to specify everything when one resorts to language in everyday situations, as one usually does in the scientific context, where the assumptions made cannot remain unstipulated. At any rate, scientific language, let alone mathematics, cannot serve as a model for the study of language in general. We should rather seek to understand, from the point of view of natural language, how scientific language is possible at all. In fact, scientific language is possible only because it presupposes natural language.

2. TOWARD AN INTEGRATED THEORY OF MEANING

2.1. *The question of the validity of the substitution view*

The substitution view of meaning discussed earlier has always seemed highly credible. It possesses the fascination of science: it seems able to show how expressions are meaningful, that is, unambiguous. Frege's analysis even presents itself as the natural explanation for certain situations that arise in everyday speech. For instance, if someone says something we do not understand and then we ask what he meant, he will reply by putting the content of his speech into other terms. He will affirm the *same thing* but in another way. In doing this, he obviously proceeds by substitution. Frege's analyses provide a theoretical account of this procedure, hence their force of persuasion. One reference, two senses, guarantee the substitutability of the expressions as well as the fact that either one of them means the other one since meaning implies substitutability. When expressions are singled out from everyday situations, e.g., when their meaning is problematical, Frege's framework, which was originally constructed to eliminate mathematical difficulties due to language and, more generally, to account for the working of univocal language by revealing the mechanisms of intelligibility, exhibits an unquestionable explanatory power. It is as if the meaning of sentences were really a function of their components (*principle of composition*) and, in the last analysis, of the referential structure of the latter (*principle of extensionality*). In virtue of those two principles, one cannot maintain that *John is tall* could mean 'My tailor is rich', even though they are both true (*one* reference: the truth-value True) and express two thoughts (*two* senses). *John* has a different reference than the noun *tailor*, and even if John were my tailor, the meaning of the predicates would still differ, in that they do not have *one* reference for the concept they express; there are tall people who are poor, and rich ones who are not tailors. The sentences containing such names could never mean one another; because they are different expressions and refer to different entities, they cannot be substituted.

But the question which necessarily arises is why names, for instance, should have a sense and a reference. Why is the sense-reference dichotomy omnipresent in language? Is it empirically observable or theoretical, and if it is theoretical, is it self-supporting, or should we rather seek for further ground upon which it is based? Why is language referential? Is it always so, and is reference an essential property of language, let alone of literature? If not, *when* is Frege's reference theory acceptable and when is it not? The answer to the last question can only be meta-Fregean since it delimits the domain in which Frege's theory applies. It pushes us toward a more integrated framework of thought lying outside the realm of the classical reference theory. Can we spell out a more general view of which Frege's would be a particular instance? At least, we should try to suggest it here and sketch some of its most general outlines.

2.2. *The problematological view of language*

In order to answer the questions raised previously, we should carefully examine why, in general, we use language. Our answer rests upon a familiar fact: human beings do what they do, whatever they do, and whenever they do it, to solve a problem which has arisen and with which they are confronted. Communicating with other people is no exception to this rule, but such communication is so natural, so unproblematic for all of us, that we hardly realize that there is a problem, akin to these we have to face in other areas of our lives. Perhaps we are too prone to associate the word *problem* with *difficulty*. But a problem cannot be reduced to an obstacle we have to overcome. More generally, anything which requires an action from us is a problem: a task to accomplish, an action to undertake, an act to perform, a difficulty to surmount, and so forth. We *need* to resolve them if we wish to achieve what we *want*. Needs, demands, and problem solving are intrinsically related to one another. An easy way to define 'problem' is to say that a problem is anything that *can* be expressed as a question or, for our purposes, an interrogative sentence.

Language is also a problem solving activity, or more strictly speaking, recourse to language is. If our relationships with other human beings were really so transparent that we could get what we wanted from them without asking that our ideas were immediately known by them as soon as they were conceived, that they were then convinced by our ideas and willing to adopt them as their own, then language would be useless. But on the top of our other problems lie these: ideas cannot pass tacitly from one mind to another, and even if they could, that passage would not imply acquiescence on the part of the other person. Language helps us surmount these difficulties: it enables us to communicate what we think, to persuade our addressee of the correctness of those thoughts, and to request cooperation in order to see that our needs and various wants are fulfilled.

If language exists insofar as it enables us to deal with our problems, it must also, to some extent, involve solutions. To use language is already a solution to some problem, even when the solution is not verbal. As a consequence, the two most fundamental functions of language are to express and reveal as such problems and solutions to problems. This implies that problems and solutions should be distinguished. Although nothing more fundamental can be said of language, one does not find many traces of this characterization in the literature on language, not even in opposition to it. It evokes rather a tacit agreement which does not raise further implications, as if the above characterization were too general and too imprecise to be useful, and permitted no systematization. Though recognized as true, it is nonetheles dispensed with. Can we not erect a consistent view of language on the basis of the question-answer relationship?[5]

Language relates us to problems: it must express them, and must then stipulate whether or not they are solved, that is, it must express solutions as well. In contrast to other problem solving techniques, language is capable of relating to all problems. This does not mean that it solves them *ipso facto*, nor does it imply that there is no *sui generis* problem that arises when recourse is made to language. But the relationship between language and what it refers to does not work in both directions. Language, in principle, covers an unlimited range of problems and is not confined to any of them in particular, while the possibilities offered by another tool are restricted to a narrow range of problems, and the solutions it permits are limited. However, the use of any tool is as specific as that of language, and the latter can seldom serve as a *substitute* for the former. In that sense, language is already a particular solution, the solution to which we resort when our problem must be referred to as a problem, or as what used to be problematic. This last difference is essential: it covers the well-known distinction between question and answer, and shows that this distinction is the most basic reality of language and derives from the very nature and function of linguistic usage. It has then to be incorporated within language itself. We now understand why the notion of a question simultaneously functions in a strictly linguistic sense (meaning 'interrogative sentence') and also exceeds the realm of sentences by having a wider application. *Question*, then, means the same as *problem*: many expressions of everyday usage refer to questions in that sense; e.g., *There is no question about it, The person in question was very rich, The question of the independence of Poland is now settled, It is a question of life and death*, and so forth. In all these examples, as in many others, we could not replace *question* by *interrogative sentence* because what is meant by *question* cannot be reduced to some linguistic *form*, but rather addresses an attitude where different alternatives are considered, even though some of them may be mentioned only to be excluded. The retro-referential case in the second example above illustrates this fact quite clearly: the word *question* is employed to identify someone by excluding everybody else who could be thought to be the person referred to.

In sum, language purports to express, and as a result, distinguish questions from answers. As this distinction is incorporated within language, it must be formally preserved. To that end, an adequate terminology must be adopted. When we resort to language in order to express our problems as such, we answer *problematologically*. When we want to stipulate their solution, we answer *apocritically* (from *apokrisis*, which means 'answer' in Greek). The difference between question and answer is then transferred to the level of explicitation, i.e. to the level of the answering function. The difference itself is not strictly speaking a matter of form. A question, or a problem, is not a solution, and vice versa. This is not a definition, but rather a formulation designed to emphasize that the difference we face here is a *pure* difference: there is no question without an answer, and vice versa. Form is subsidiary, a *means* to encapsulate tha difference. Questions and answers are known entities to all of us, human beings as we are, and do not raise any further question. But if you really do not know what a question is, just ask, and then you will necessarily know *ex post facto*. As to solutions, they end the problem solving activity partially or for a certain length of time, and, as a result, the problem vanishes if it had even arisen at all.

More important than the nature of the *problematological difference*, as I call it, are its implications. The problem-answer complex is our starting point. Its linguistic version, the 'question-answer complex', is itself a derivation, and I am not sure that it is a linguistic duality at all. A question may be identified as an interrogative sentence, but 'to be an answer' is not in itself a linguistic category. In sum, *either* we express problems, because we expect a solution from the persons to whom we address ourselves, *or* we *propose* the solutions in telling them what we think of those problems on the assumption that these persons share, or will share, the problems in question, i.e. the preoccupations raised by what we have said.

In both cases, we respond to the problems we must face: partially, in the former situation, and totally, in the latter. Therefore, in the latter case, the problem disappears, while in the first case, it comes to be expressed as a problem. We shall call the expression of a problem the *problematological answer*, and its solution, the *apocritical answer*. A problematological answer is a partial answer to the problem raised, for to express a problem to someone else from whom we expect the solution is already a step towards its complete resolution: how could the interlocutor respond to what we want if we did not tell him what we wanted? Language is thus made up of two kinds of answers which enable its users to question and to respond, or at least, to express questions and solutions, transferring this essential difference to language itself. It may sound awkward to regard answers, albeit problematologically, as functioning as question bearers and as problem indicators. In fact, they are answers with respect to the Wittgensteinian forms of life, but within language, they import problems as such. And as such, they are expressions of problems, and are literally problematological (from *logos* and *problema*). Language, as a human attribute, incorporates the difference between problems and solutions from the human exigencies of everyday life. Language can express them all and, at the same time, must functionally respect this difference, if only by focusing on one or the other of its components. In other words, each expression can be seen as problematological as well as apocritical, and any distinction between the two emerges only from the context. If I say *Now I ask you, what's the matter with kids nowadays*, it may be seen as a mere apocritical answer uttered to declare something to somebody else in the guise of information (*What do you say? → I ask you What's the matter with kids nowadays*), or as a problematological answer responding to the speaker's *problem, for instance, of knowing* what X thinks of something (kids nowadays). Problematologically, this answer is a problem indicator rather than a sentence indicative of its solution. Declarative sentences are generally used as apocritical indicating devices, though in the context chosen above, the declarative sentence functions as problem conveying. By itself or in itself, a sentence is therefore apocritical and problematological: this fact also accounts for rhetorical questions which are disguised assertions. A sentence, therefore, contains both elements and they are always distinguishable. They must be if someone other than the speaker needs to identify the problem he or she has to solve for the speaker, or if the addressee must identify what is rendered explicit by the speaker as the latter's opinion on a definite, though implicit, question which is supposed to be of mutual interest.

We should be careful not to amalgamate problems and solutions with, respectively, interrogative and non-declarative sentences. I do not claim a link does not exist there, but it is looser than one might think at first sight. We should rather see problems as questions and solutions as answers. A question, when raised *explicitly*, often becomes what people usually call a question: a written sentence or phrase followed by a question mark or pronounced with a *characteristic* intonation. A question lies beyond these surface markings and is in fact the problem raised by its explicit manifestation as an expression.

The problematological difference, as I call it, is essential for the purpose of identification I mentioned above and must therefore be respected. It institutes the double function of language with respect to the forms of life. There are many ways in which questions are distinguished from answers. One way is to stipulate apocritically the question solved in the assertion: what the proposition is about, what is in question in what is said, is explicit and no more confusion can arise in this case than in the situation where the question answered by the proposition was left implicit. People use language because they have a problem in mind, to be expressed or resolved. In any case, they speak or write in reference to that problem, even when it is left unexpressed and implicit. The problematological difference is *formally* respected (declarative sentences versus non-declarative ones) in a given context: declarative sentences assert something about a certain question, and function as its solution. The question is 'in' the answer if the answer has a meaning, since the answer says something about the question it deals with as its topic. But the question remains implicit in that given context: it is absently present. It could be made explicit, but then it would be explicitly identifiable as a question, i.e. would be presented as *different* from its solution. *This is the most basic and most essential consequence of the presence of the question-answer complex in language.* If declarative sentences are used for the assertion of solutions, non-declarative sentences will be used (but it is not their only use) to indicate problems.

The problematological difference also ensues if the question the proposition deals with is stipulated. But the opposition explicit/implicit, as formulated earlier, may be sufficient: the question, once solved, is not mentioned because it is not the goal of the questioning process to mention it; its goal is to affirm the solution. If a speaker asserts a proposition, no wonder he does not mention to his addressee — who is supposed to know — what the question was. The opposition of form is also a good means to characterize the difference if the question must nonetheless be stipulated as such.

A third way is to specify the question, so that no confusion can possibly arise. It can be done merely by saying what the question is or was. But this is only a particularization of a more general procedure: the question can be specified in various ways, and one of these plays a fundamental role. One can always render explicit the question dealt with in the answer or the question solved by it. To render a question explicit *as such*, whatever the means employed in our use of language, is always done in view of avoiding the problematological confusion which consists in recognizing no difference or allowing no difference to be recognized between questions and answers. Since both entities can be expressed through assertions, such a confusion is quite possible; sometimes because no expressed stipulation of what counts as a question and what counts as an answer is made by the speaker. But even in the case where the question is marked within the assertion, the global answer, though stipulating the original question, can answer another one in virtue of its apocritical autonomy. There is, however, a fundamental phenomenon revealed by what we could call *interrogative expansion.*

2.3. *The problematological theory of reference*

Propositions, being answers, are related to the questions that gave rise to them: what is in question in what is said is called the *meaning*, and the question dealt with indicates the topic of the discourse. In other words, one always views a discourse in the context of a question which specifies what the discourse is about, that is, what is literally in question. Once the question is resolved, there is no need to mention it again, unless, of course, one needs to recall it, for instance, when one does not understand what had been said, or more generally, when the speaker wants to make explicit what had been in question (and was resolved) in what he said (i.e. in the global answer). In the latter case, the process at work is linked with the necessities of intelligibility: the speaker takes precautions by resorting to an *interrogative expansion* that glosses the terms which could be or actually are problematic, presenting them *in reference to* what is or could appear in question. This expansion gives birth to what grammarians call a relative clause, which has the foreseen effect of ascribing a definite reference, if not some possible definition, to the term *in question.*

Let us consider one example:

(1)   Napoleon lost at Waterloo.

This sentence means the same as:

(2)   Napoleon is the individual *who* lost at Waterloo.

It also means:

(3)   Napoleon is he *who* did something *which* is . . . at a place *where* . . .

Interrogatives are used as pronouns in order to introduce those clauses: they naturally refer back to the question which could arise or did arise concerning the meaning of the terms employed. Thus, the process of interrogative expansion can be theoretically infinite, or could, at any rate, continue until all the words in the language had appeared somewhere in the interrogative expansion.

In what sense is what we have here a reference theory, and how does it differ from the classical reference theory developed by Frege?

Referentiality is an essential property of language: it enables its users not to know what reality *is*, as some philosophers used to claim before Wittgenstein, but to know *how* human beings can relate to reality, i.e. which terms *can* let us know something empirical, something that can be found outside language. Whether that something has existence, whether it is an individual entity or not, are questions that cease to concern the theory of referentiality, since that theory addresses only the nature of what is referred to. The theory of language has often been misconceived since Russell as an ontology, and more precisely, as an ontology at the service of empiricist prejudices. Even the terminology currently employed betrays the allegiance to empiricism when philosophers speak of 'reference' instead of referentiality. References are what is referred to by referential terms (the so-called 'logically proper names'). We shall continue to use the traditional terminology, but with the aforementioned reservations in mind. We do not have to inquire into the nature of reference here, but should simply ask how it is that reference is marked within answers and by what means that relationship with 'the world', whatever the latter consists of, is rendered possible.

The solution to that problem reveals itself to us in the light of examples (1), (2), and (3) given above. These examples lend themselves to an immediate generalization. The terms we have brought into play in (1) are successively defined in (2) and (3) thanks to relative clauses introduced by interrogatives which specify what was in question. The interrogative expansion is assertorical in the sense that it closes the question introduced, i.e., it offers a resolution to the question previously raised or considered answered. The interrogative, on the other hand, has a precise function when used in the mode of assertion (though it has the same one in interrogative sentences): it refers to something. What answers the clause *who lost at Waterloo* if not Napoleon? But we should be careful with the use of italics. What is referred to in the incomplete expression *who lost at Waterloo*? It is a term or a man that saturates it? In other words, does the reference theory provide a more fundamental way of explaining how judgments are formed and why they are semantically basic in a theory of language as units of thought than the theory advanced here? Or, on the contrary, has the reference theory nothing to do with it, the theory's only aim being to account for our relationship to the world as a theory of what we call semantics in vernacular language? As the exegetes of Frege pointed out, it is unclear which term of the alternative Frege opted for. The debate has thus remained open.

Before tackling the problem of expressing referred entities within language, of quoting them, and of mentioning them, let us return to our interrogative clauses.

2.3.1. The expression *who lost at Waterloo* is incomplete. It could be taken for a question in a given context, in which intonation and/or punctuation make the (problematological) difference. As such, however, it is nothing more than a referring *expression* in need of a term to which, precisely, it would refer, i.e. which would *answer* the description. When such a term is supplied, we have a full answer in reference to the question mentioned, raised, or underlying the language use, and the interrogative *who* naturally disappears, becoming then superfluous. In other words, if the referring expression above was considered as a question, the answer would be *Napoleon* or *Napoleon lost at Waterloo*. Quite clearly, this referring expression – when it is not used as a question but as a means to identify the person (in question) who lost at Waterloo – gives rise to a proposition in which the interrogative is deleted: we cannot consider *Napoleon who lost at Waterloo* as a complete, meaningful expression. The interrogative must be suppressed, and only then do we have a well-formed proposition: *Napoleon lost at Waterloo*. This analysis clearly reveals how propositions are formed and why, even syntactically, they should be considered as answers. The questions to which they answer need not be explicitly posed: one does not have to ask explicitly *Who lost at Waterloo?* in order to utter the proposition *Napoleon lost at Waterloo,* though we would never utter this proposition if, somehow, there was no question as to *who* lost that battle (or as to *what* happened there – in this case the question bears on the predicate), if, in some way, there was no question at stake. We could also say that the statement *Napoleon lost at Waterloo* bears upon a definite question, though this is not apparent from the statement itself, since it merely *asserts* something. The statement surely deals with some question or other, about which it says what it says. The person in question, the fact in question, or the event in question in that judgment give us the various interrogatives which could appear if those questions were posed explicitly: *Who lost the battle of Waterloo?, What did Napoleon do at Waterloo?, What happened at Waterloo?* The terms which appear in a proposition may, therefore, be considered as answers to the interrogatives and to their corresponding interrogative clauses. As they answer the interrogatives, the latter are deleted or are simply superfluous. The questions which could arise remain present in some manner, albeit tacitly, since such term in the proposition represents and proleptically satisfies a question. This is the origin of the *wh*-questions: they are the questions which could be raised about those terms, which would problematize them, and whose answer would also define them in some manner. The absence of these interrogatives merely signifies that they are not problematic, that what they indicate is clear or deemed to be clear. Their reference does not need to be elucidated, and the proposition containing them acquires some semantical autonomy. *What* is affirmed is *known* and deemed to be known. No further question arises as to *what* is said, and therefore, no interrogative appears to determine what is in question and to show that the proposition solves it by saying what it says. Of course, if questions had to arise about the terms involved – subject or predicate – we would have *wh*-questions, as in examples (2) or (3). The terms of a proposition appear to have a *saturation* function with respect to the *wh*-words. To the terms of the proposition corresponds a possible *wh*-question which has been solved, or could be considered as having been solved. It may sound odd for a proposition to have as underlying structure a set of questions which are treated without having ever been actually asked. From the point of view of the analysis of the proposition, however, we can say that, in (1) for instance, the question of Napoleon and of a battle lost is at stake; what is in question seems to be some event which consisted in Napoleon's defeat. Besides, if the proposition (1) does not convey its own intelligibility, the terms can be defined with the help of referring expressions introduced with interrogatives used in the mode of assertion (i.e. as relative clauses), corresponding to the respective *wh*-questions. Undoubtedly, then, *wh*-words give rise to those terms and, as we shall see, to the whole proposition; since the *wh*-words thereby become superfluous, they are deleted. The terms are supposed to be literally understandable within the proposition; their reference is supposed to be known and should not need to be specified through interrogative expansion. One therefore knows what answers to these unproblematic terms.

But quite clearly, the fact that those *wh*-questions *could* arise does not mean that the speaker ever raised them in order to produce his final proposition. The conjecture we put forth in the light of our analysis of (1), (2), and (3) is that some question must have been dealt with, at least implicitly. The problematological conception of language, however, clearly stipulates that there is no utterance, no proposition, without there being some question(s) associated with it in the mind of its author that he wants to treat by resorting to language. The fact that this problem (or these questions) has (have) not been explicitly posed is not an objection against our view. The purpose of raising a question is not to see it duplicated, but to express its resolution, and if that resolution is linguistic, then, quite clearly, what will be uttered is the resolution and not the question. One does not offer the resolution to a problem by saying "This is a problem" when one can assert its resolution and can thereby *eliminate* what was problematic as such. It is little wonder, then, that we respond to our problems without raising them as such or that we find our problems referred back to in their corresponding resolution. The propositions will therefore be apocritical, without saying that they are; they implicitly refer back to the questions which have arisen for the speaker and for which he literally *proposes* a resolution.

To sum up: the interrogative clause of (2) provides the meaning of the term *Napoleon.* The interrogative refers to Napoleon as the individual who answers the description introduced by the interrogative.

2.3.2. We now know why interrogatives have a referential function: their mission is to enable us to identify *what* is in question, *what* we speak of, *what* answers to the terms contained in our language. Terms, subjects, and predicates have a reference because they saturate the *wh*-words that correspond to them. They would appear explicitly if some problem arose as to their meaning. These terms stand for the interrogatives and the fact that the latter are deleted or simply absent indicates that no further question arises in the mind of the speaker as to what these terms denote.

However, we have still ignored the process by which the problematological reference theory accounts for the combination of terms into judgments or propositions. The classical reference theory of Frege and Russell provided an answer, or rather two contradictory ones. Frege's theory was based on the assumption that names and predicates were necessary to one another for semantical reasons: names do not mean anything in isolation, no more than predicates do, but only acquire meaning through being joined. This was Frege's argument to explain why a proposition is the basic unit of thought and meaning. This did not prevent him, however, from affirming that names and predicates have a sense and a reference by themselves. If we agree to be consistent, we must add a corollary: names, as well as predicates, must have a signification, a meaning, by themselves. Why, then, should they be combined into judgments? Frege's attitude was inspired by the following necessity: to render impossible the substitutability of judgments referring to the same truth-value and expressing *two* thoughts which were obviously semantically irreducible, such as *John is tall* and *The grass is green.* The principle of composition requires that names be analyzed, and the principle of extensionality, that the respective references of those names be compared. *John* does not *mean*, i.e. is not identical to or substitutable for 'grass', since the references of *John* and *grass* are not identical. The substitutability of propositions must presuppose that of the names they contain. And this, in turn, implies that names have both sense and reference, i.e. meaning. The principle of composition, together with the principle of extensionality, constitutes the backbone of the *classical reference theory*. Its purpose is to explain why sentences are intelligible, even when their surface structure may be ambiguous. Intelligibility implies *one* meaning. A given sentence is 'intelligible' if some logical meaning is implicit in its surface structure. We all know that if someone asks us what we mean by something we have just said, we shall reply with one proposition which is meant to be equivalent. This logical equivalence is the secret of intelligibility, and Frege wanted to capture it using his two principles. On the one hand, names can be deprived of reference, and perhaps *should* be if their encapsulation within judgments is to make sense at all. On the other hand, names must have a reference if the whole mechanism of substitution is to hold at all. Judgments as semantical units only exist if the two principles above are valid, i.e. if names are referential, and such judgments do not have to be made if names have a reference. Those principles imply that propositions must be considered in the light of the reference of the names embodied in those propositions. Such principles, and more particularly the principles of composition, make judgments possible as such. The Reference Theory does account for the existence and necessity of a broader unit than the name *once we have already granted that such a unit as the proposition exists*. That is why the propositional theory is the background and the presupposition of the classical reference theory: it is only because sentences are meaningful *per se* that names are meaningful and consequently have a reference. Nevertheless, if names have a reference, one cannot see why they would be semantically incomplete to such an extent that they would have to be encapsulated within statements. If names and predicates have a sense and a reference, one cannot see where their identity breaks down and where their necessary complementarity appears. It could be in what they denote, but then, we are committed to a *petitio principii* to answer the question: How are propositions, i.e. judgments, possible? Judgments may have a different function, but since they are both referential and 'senseful', that difference must lie outside of sense and reference; and the classical reference theory must then be declared incomplete.

Russell was more consistent in this respect. He said that names that are logically entitled to be called names must be referential, and that a name must have a reference if it has a sense. But propositions can refer to other propositions, can *mention* them, and, in turn, can be mentioned by other propositions. The postulate of a hierarchy of types was erected by Russell in order to enable the language analyst to establish a difference between names standing for propositions, so to speak, and names standing for objects (as names all should in the last analysis, according to the empiricist view of Russell's *axiom of reductibility*). This axiom seems useless in mathematics and even seemed theoretically absurd to Gödel as an exigency of language. After all, mathematicians do not refer to empirical objects, and even if they could, it would be useless to always try to find an empirical content for the notions they bring to the fore. In Russell's theory, names always have reference, and the principle of composition, which postulates their analysis, becomes the principle of the hierarchy of types. The principle of extensionality, then, becomes in Russell's theory the axiom of reductibility. The main objections to this version of the principle of composition that attempt to avoid Frege's dilemma about names are well-known. First, a name that does stand for a proposition does not really differ from a description. Second, Russell's theory leads to the infinite regression that Wittgenstein has often described in his demand that language have semantical immanence. If a proposition, to be understandable and meaningful, must be defined in terms of a metaproposition, and this higher type, in turn, to be intelligible, needs to be seen in terms of a third type, and so on, we shall have to go outside language in order to understand *this* proposition at all. Hence Wittgenstein said that a proposition had to *show* its meaning, rather then *say* it; if one *had* to say it in order to grasp its meaning, one would have to use another proposition to say what the meaning of the first one was. And so for the second proposition. We would fall back into Russell's infinite regression. A proposition *can,* of course, be used to mention the meaning of another proposition, but it does not have to; language must be logical in and of itself. Otherwise, one *would* have to regress indefinitely from proposition to proposition to understand just *one* of them, and finally get out of language to discover how it functions. The unspeakable is an uncomfortable standpoint from which to discuss language. It is contradictory and absurd to *affirm* that the appropriate way of *speaking* about language is to go outside of it, i.e. where we cannot speak at all. The implication is that language must reveal its underlying structure through its surface structure. Perhaps this explains why Wittgenstein found his own reconstructionist enterprise in the *Tractatus* so contradictory in its aim to show that language need not be logically reconstructed. To *say* what is to be *shown*, to say what *cannot* or ought not to be said, because it requires us to go outside of language to see the whole of it (and outside language, there is only that which cannot be said: silence would be the truth of language, the key to a proper discussion of it) was eventually deemed contradictory by Wittgenstein himself, who rejected his endeavors to encapsulate language within the logical theory of the proposition.

2.3.3. We have just seen that the classical reference theory was unable to answer the question 'How are judgments possible?' It presupposes the validity of propositional theory, which considers propositions as the basic units of intelligibility, right from the start instead of explaining it. Hence its commitment to some principle of composition which we have proved cannot be retained whatever its form. Wittgenstein himself rejected his propositional theory as developed in the *Tractatus*, but retained one of its versions (not the logicist one, however) by adhering to the immanence of meaning of individual sentences. In his *Investigations*, he analyzes individual, isolated propositions, thereby legitimating one of the most fallacious practices (i.e. sentence truncation) of so-called *linguistic philosophy*.

How does the problematological reference theory answer the question 'How are judgments possible?'

Judgments or propositions arise from the need to deal with questions we have in mind, i.e. to answer them. They are uttered or written as functions of those questions and in *response* to them. But they are generally the only visible results of this association since the questions, once answered, cease to be and disappear, even if they had once been mentioned. This does not imply that no trace of them remains. The fact that *Napoleon lost at Waterloo* means 'Napoleon is the individual *who* lost at Waterloo' is quite illuminating in this respect. When a question about something arises, *what* is in question demands to be answered, and answered in such a way that what was in question becomes out-of-the-question. As a result, a proposition emerges. That proposition is the answer to the question; it need contain the questionable as being not questionable anymore, that is, it must contain a term that renders the problematic non-problematic. The term in question may be either one of what tradition calls the subject and the predicate; either way, the term that expresses the concern of the question raised must be supplemented with a term and a relative clause to which it answers, a clause which must be deleted. The process of deletion gives rise to another term, and hence to the judgment. An answer, thus, is made of at least two elements: the questionable and the unquestionable, both appearing at the level of the answer as a now-out-of-the-question. The combination of those two question-related entities make up the global answer to the question, i.e. the proposition that states *what* was in question as being solved. We now understand why we have a subject and a predicate in a proposition or a proper name and a description: those two components are as complementary to each other as the question and what answers the question. But what answers the question cannot simply be put forward. It refers back to the question, to what was in question and indicates that (and how) the question is resolved. Hence all judgments are to be considered as answers. For instance, we could answer *Who lost at Waterloo?* with *Napoleon,* but this is shorthand for the full proposition *Napoleon lost at Waterloo* (cf. the expressions *Yes* and *Yes, I do.*) Consequently, it is equally true (a) to say that *Napoleon* answers the description *the man who lost at Waterloo* or *x lost at Waterloo* if we prefer to take into account the deletion process and regard the *who* as an assertoric *referring indicator* of someone yet to be discovered, (b) and to say that *Napoleon* is the problematic term to be answered (*Who is Napoleon?*), and *the man who lost at Waterloo* is the answer term (or term group). In virtue of the complementarity emphasized above, we have *Napoleon* and *x who lost at Waterloo*, or *Napoleon (is) x and x lost at Waterloo*, which becomes *Napoleon (x who) lost at Waterloo.* Either the subject or the predicate gives the name of what is problematic and that which is, as such, in need of an answer through an answer term (or group term), i.e. in need of another expression referring to what is problematic, but involving it now as non-problematic. Both terms refer to the same 'what', and thus refer to the same entity. Subjects and predicates relate to the same reality in the world, albeit in a different manner.

2.3.4. *Reference and its mention*

To what does the word 'reference' actually refer? Is it another name for reality, or does it denote what corresponds to expressions that identify or refer? We should at least be aware that this is a difficulty, though one very seldom alluded to, in reference theory. To shed some light on the problem, we should pursue the consequences following from each of those two alternatives.

In the first alternative, reference is defined as the portion of reality covered by the term used to denote it. Napoleon is the reference of *Napoleon* a proper name, and of *the man who lost at Waterloo*, a description, in which *lost at Waterloo* is the predicate. Names and predicates both refer to the same individual, i.e. in our example, to Napoleon Bonaparte. With this conception of reference, the difference between names and predicates begins to vanish. As a result, it cannot explain why a name is necessary and hence why judgments should arise and form the minimal semantic unit since a predicate is already a referring expression in many cases. And, as we know, one of the aims of the classical reference theory was to provide a basis for the propositional theory. In what sense are predicative referring expressions incomplete?

A proposition like *John is tall* gives us the answer. *To be tall* refers to John, but how could we know what, or who exactly, is tall if we did not have a term to tell us that it is John. Once again, John is referred to by both the name *John* and, in this example, by the predicate *is tall*. Reference is obviously the key for understanding why a judgment, i.e. a two-term entity with an indi-vidualized referring term (the subject), is necessary. This explains why Frege had always wanted to make a distinction between the various functions of the word *being*, i.e. the copula. In (1), *Napoleon lost at Waterloo*, we face some kind of identity; however, in *John is tall*, *is* obviously has some other function. We are nevertheless tempted to say that (1) is also a judgment, involving the use of a copulative expression, so that Frege's reservations may appear *ad hoc*.

(4)   John is tall

can, like (1), be expanded along the same lines into (5), and for the same reason:

(5)   John is the man *who* is tall.

This explanation obviously implies that the interrogative clause enables the addressee to know exactly who the man is, i.e. that the clause in question ren-ders him identifiable. This will not work if, for example, there is more than one tall man in the place in question, or if the precise place is not exactly known by the receiver of the message.

At any rate, we may ask ourselves, for (1) and (2), as much as for (4) and (5), why a subject term is needed. If we say *the individual who lost the battle at Waterloo*, we know that the one referred to by that expression is unique. Why, then, should we need a logical subject to form a sentence that functions as a selection device in the class of items that the predicate may refer to? The same applies to (4) and (5): when we say *the man who is tall*, if John is the referred individual covered by the expression, and if the expression makes that known to the hearer, then the term *John* seems superfluous. Of course, we could always argue that there is only *one* battle that took place at Waterloo and that only one person lost it, whereas several persons can be tall. But we could also say that Napoleon is not *the* man who lost at Waterloo, but that many others from Grouchy to Fabrice del Dongo lost that battle in the same place. On the other hand, we could affirm that the predicative expression *who is tall* refers quite specifically to one individual in the context of its utterance, as much as the predicate *who lost at Waterloo* refers to one particular individual. *Who* is in question in (5) and (2) is made completely known through the predicate: this is deemed to be so by the speaker, so much so that specifying the subject of the sentence adds no further information. I can say *The man who lost at Waterloo was an Emperor*, without *having* to add who he was, i.e. Napoleon-who-did-so-and-so. I can say *The tall man is now drinking a glass of wine*, since I assume right from the start that, *over there, that* tall man is someone identifiable. Why should we add *John*?

Moreover, if *Napoleon* refers to the same individual as *the man who lost the battle of Waterloo*, why do we not write *Napoleon* is *the man who lost at Waterloo*, since it is a fact that both refer to the same entity in reality, which renders their predicative coupling possible and necessary.

In the second alternative described above, we require of the reference theory an explanation for the necessity of forming judgments. With (2), for example, we are tempted to say that the relative clause refers to Napoleon: we can identify him, describe him, refer to him thanks to the predicative expression, just as we can identify John in (4). The interrogative clause, then, refers, as an expanded predicate, to the subject of the whole sentence, which must be supplied in order to get a complete description of the reality involved. And this, of course, might imply that names could denote nothing at all.

We nonetheless continue to be tempted to say that interrogative clauses, which, when they are not accidental, are strict referring expressions (*John, who is tall, drinks a glass of wine* is a good example of such an accidental clause), in fact refer to the subjects of the sentences in which they appear.

At any rate, we remain confronted with a dilemma. *The man who lost at Waterloo* is supposed to denote Napoleon; this gives us the subject of our full sentence, *Napoleon is the man who lost* . . . Do we write Napoleon or *Napoleon*? If Napoleon is the portion of reality denoted by the predicative expression, then we should write *Napoleon*, since we then only have a name for this denoted reality. Why should we even use a name since the referring expression does the job of letting us know who we are talking about? We should write [*Napoleon* is *the man who lost* . . .], but we do not want to say that a name lost the battle but an individual; so when we write *Napoleon is the man who lost* . . . , instead of [*Napoleon* is *the man* . . .], Napoleon is not a name, in spite of appearances, but an individual.

The problematological conception of reference can help us to see through all this. A predicative expression with or without an interrogative requires a subject. The absence of interrogatives only reveals that the process is completed, as we have seen earlier. We then have sentences like (1) instead of (2). The process of formation deserves careful study. Underlying sentences like (1) and (4) are questions. What is in question needs to be answered. Let us suppose that who lost the battle of Waterloo is in question. Then, Napoleon is the answer. Is the word *Napoleon* just used to designate the individual we mean by that word? No, *Napoleon* is clearly an *answer*. Formally, we have the following steps:

(6)   *Who lost the battle of Waterloo?*   is the question.

(7)   *Napoleon*   is the answer.

As we now know from the problematological conception, an answer does not refer to itself *qua* answer and does not render explicit that it is an answer, but simply specifies *what* it answers. And this is how reference (as that which the particle *what* reveals) comes in. The goal of producing an answer is not to stipulate that it is an answer but to say something else. This explains why language is referential, that is, turned towards reality external to itself. Just as the question need not be stipulated, so it goes for the answer too; (6) and (7) become:

(6´)   *Who lost at Waterloo?*

(7´)   *Napoleon*

or

(7´´)   Napoleon lost at Waterloo.

(7´´) is preferred to (7´) if we want to stress that *what* was in question is now answered. *It is because neither question nor answer refer to themselves as such* that *in the last analysis we have a subject, and consequently, a full proposition.*

Only *what* is in question appears, and therefore, *what* is answered also appears, without having to be stipulated as having been questioned or having given rise to a corresponding answer: this is how reference (i.e. *whatness*) emerges.

If we consider proposisions in themselves and develop a componential analysis, we are bound to encounter the difficulties with the reference theory cited previously. A proposition is the closure of a dynamic of thought, one which we cannot adequately deal with if we approach it through its final step. We must link that proposition with what is in question in *what* is said, with the question that deletes itself insofar as it says *what* it says. Deletion of interrogatives is only one of the manifestations of the question disappearing into the answer. The whole question-answer complex disappears then as such, and the answer shows only *what* it says, its content (or meaning), its reference. This process requires that we constantly make a distinction that founds the judgment. In this light, it is clear that a judgment *is basically a complementary difference between two items, a subject and a predicative expression in order to express something as being the object of a solution.*

2.4. *Reference and meaning*

The connection between meaning and reference is so intricate that in German, for instance, one uses the same word for both notions. Is there something more fundamental beyond the mere play of words which explains the interrelatedness of meaning and reference? The answer to this question cannot easily be found in Frege's writings. The *rationale* of such a link can be seen in the fact that we must resort to interrogatives, as we shall see in the next section, when the stipulation of meaning is requested. When they are used for that purpose, interrogatives indicate the reference of some term, thereby supplying some definiton for it, at least as a presupposed (propositional) content. The employment of interrogatives in a referential manner is only one mode of introducing questioning into language. But the interesting fact in all of this is that the assertions of reference theory are predictable consequences of the problematological conception of language. When interrogatives are deleted, it is because the questions which are to be treated are considered – rightly or wrongly, but this is not the point – as solved: the terms in question are deemed to be completely specified. This means that what they refer to does not raise any question at all in the eyes of the speaker. The world they describe, so to speak, is known as much as is necessary, and does not have to be inquired into further for the expressions at work to receive their full content and specification. If, for instance, one did not know exactly who Napoleon was, what the battle in question was, and what losing it meant in terms of its effect on the world, questions about them would arise and answers like (2) and (3), instead of (1), would be offered to the addressee.

In other terms, if a word like Waterloo did not mean anything to the hearer, if he did not know *what* Waterloo was, i.e. what is referred to by that name, the hearer would necessarily, according to our view, receive an answer involving an interrogative expansion of the word *Waterloo*, specifying what is in question in the use of this word, that is, the *reference* of the word in question (as having been questionable). When, on the contrary, the speaker does without such an expansion and utters a sentence like (1), for instance, he thereby reveals that, in his mind, the reference of the terms employed is sufficiently known to the hearer for him or her to understand what *is in question*, what the sentence and the terms involved are about. The utterance of (1) presupposes that the references are literally out-of-the question and therefore need not be referred back to that question through some interrogative.

One could argue that it is empirical evidence which, as we have just seen, determines the fact that the knowledge of reference gives meaning. And this, as we have relentlessly argued, is a limitative view of meaning, one that is also based on a reference theory which is not deprived of contradictions. It follows from our discussion that the classical reference theory, as such, does not hold. It must be seen in the light of a more general framework: the problematological reference theory, which imposes itself as a grounding framework as soon as we realize that reference is always stipulated in terms of interrogatives. Frege's conception of reference now appears as a special case of a general process and therefore cannot be taken as valid for all cases of meaning. Hence our question concerns the limits of validity of any reference theory offered as an explanation of what meaning really consists of. If we want to understand why some terms have a reference which, when specified, indicates their meaning *and* allows for substitution between sentences, we must appeal to a broader conception than Frege's *and* delimit the domain in which Frege's conception may appear adequate. In that broader framework, meaning is an essential feature of questioning, one that cannot be restricted to reference *simply because questioning, in its very nature, is not always a referential process.* The referential use of *interrogative indicators* is only one among many possible usages of questions. The mere existence of unintelligible literary works suggests that meaning will in many cases be something other than an equivalent statement and will therefore be unable to undergo a Fregean treatment. The substitution view grounded in the classical reference theory systematized by Frege has a limited range of applicability. Besides, we definitely expect a reference theory of meaning, whatever its restricted range of meaningfulness, to provide *theoretical grounds* for asserting that, in the cases foreseen by the theory, reference equals meaning. Frege's presentation of the association of meaning with reference often seems to be a merely empirical phenomenon. Meaning must be reinserted within the general theory of questioning.

2.5. *From substitutions to questions*

Interrogatives are used when predicates must be understood as well as when names need explication. *This explains why subjects as well as predicates have a reference.* Questioning enables us to relate to the world through the employment of language. This relationship to the world is called referentiality when it involves designation or denomination. The world, things, or whatever we decide to call reality, are not *given* to us but must be specified and can only emerge to us as such as a result of a process of research. This process most often leads to 'finding' what we already know. Continuity is then an intrinsic feature of our relationship to the world. But it also permits us to discover *what* we did not know previous to that query. In other words, we must look for reality in order to reach it, for it to force itself upon us *as reality*. Questioning is the constitutive process of the appearances. What can appear and which is real only appears as a result of questioning.

Questions, as we have seen, are present in language in various ways, all of them deriving from a more fundamental reality of questioning that language must translate. As a result, language is referential through terms which are all so referentially overdetermined that no question arises about them. Such terms are known in logic and grammar as subjects and predicates. The problematological conception of reference does not mean to provide any ontology. What is referred to cannot be specified and does not need to be. This theory does not allow us to tell what reality is made of, but only to affirm that our language, via its terms, has a referential function linked to questioning. However, because questioning is now the measure of reference, we should understand the latter notion in a specific way, one distinct from what we traditionally mean by the word *reference*. Interrogatives designate what counts. Nothing proves that something outside language corresponds to the term used to answer what is in question. The interrogative only gives us indications of *what* to look for.

The problematological reference theory differs from the classical one by dissociating meaning and reference on the ground that they are linked only in specific cases. This linkage *does not essentially matter when it comes to specifying what meaning is in general.* The core of the classical reference theory is that reference is *given* with terms, and *thereby* meaning exists when *terms* are at work within propositions. In fact, references, as denoted individual and empirical items, are not given with terms and propositions, but let themselves be known as a result of a questioning process ending in answers. They appear as given when the dynamic of questioning is completed, both for the speaker and his audience. When the questions raised concern objects and things, reference is objectual in the narrow sense of the word. But these kinds of questions are far from being the only ones. As a consequence, the objects of inquiry are not necessarily physical entities, and a theory of reference which only allows for empiricism appears overly limiting. The problematological framework, on the contrary, presents only a minimal requirement as to how reference is to be understood: *what* is in question receives a determination; the question ceases to be a question, and *what* was in question then appears within some answer as being that to which the answer refers because the answer specifies *what* it is (in some sense or other of the word *is*, one that may be, for instance, copulative or existential). This explains why the question is in the answer: *what* is in question, the specific question, and that which is questionable are the same reality, which, when it ceases to be problematic, is nonetheless present in its apocritical determination as being no longer questionable in terms of the *what*-question that had previously determined it. *What* is said about it specifies *what* it is in some way or another. Reference is specified as a result of a questioning process, in which the answer presents as known the objects of the questions raised previously; therefore, what was in question becomes identified in its *whatness*. There is a dynamic of specification where the *whatness* of the questionable disappears as questionable and emerges as stipulative (e.g. through relative clauses introduced by assertoric interrogatives as in *What you said is interesting.*)

That is the minimal and sole exigency of the problematological reference theory, and it obviously does exclude answering that *whatness* in objectual, empirically oriented terms, such as Russell's proper names. But, in our view, reference is defined as a result of the saturating and deletion process of hypothetical or underlying interrogatives or questions which can be posed via those interrogatives.

At this point, we can make a further distinction which will shed light on what has just been said. There is no difference between a question and what is in question, i.e. its object, so to speak. If one says that the question is whether it will rain tomorrow, one can also say that *what* is *in* question is whether it will rain tomorrow, and one can also say that the object of the question is tomorrow's rain. Tomorrow's rain is the question. The distinction we have to make is the following: something is in question and that fact constitutes the question, or something is in question and that is *not* the question. In the former case, we face a problem of reference. The answer will have to stipulate the reference. In the latter case, the object of the question *is not* that something but is *about* that something.

In both cases, however, the reference is further determined. In the first case, it is exclusively determined. In the second, we quite obviously do not have a question of reference: reference is probably already settled in the mind of the interrogator. Hence the answer here is not directly definitional. However, we must remember that answers are always indirectly definitional since what is in question is still referred to. In (1), for instance, what is in question is the battle of Waterloo. But (1) may perfectly well have been uttered in response to *Who lost at Waterloo?* This shows that the question which (1) answers does not have to be equated with what is in question in (1). We then say that (1) is *about* the battle of Waterloo: something is said about it, namely that Napoleon lost it. Indirectly, as we have said, one then knows *who* Napoleon is or was, although the question does not bear directly on the reference of the name *Napoleon* as in *Who was Napoleon?*. In *Napoleon lost at Waterloo*, what is in question is not necessarily who Napoleon was although Napoleon is in question in whatever is answered about him.

Let us consider the relationship between meaning and reference. According to a well-established tradition, to mean is to refer. When we ask for the meaning of a term, the answer directly supplies the reference of that term. However, such a response is only valid in the contexts considered by the propositional theory of meaning. It does not hold for fictional discourse in particular or for all types of discourse in general, as soon as we realize that to understand meaning we do not *analyze* it term by term, but rather grasp it as a whole in its textuality. The fact that meaning and reference are associated must then be seen as accidental, as a surface phenomenon. The relationship between meaning and reference reflects a deeper level of phenomena, one that involves questioning. The problematological theory of meaning can account for what the propositional theory explains, but the propositional theory cannot account for what the problematological theory explains. Even when both theories are examined on equal terms, careful study shows that in language questions are involved, interrogatives emerge, and reference *thereby* becomes specified for all the terms of the single proposition in question. Meaning and reference are undoubtedly linked, but this linkage is a result of something more basic, something that had not been perceived by those who noticed that in many cases — cases that they were too prompt to generalize into an overall conception — meaning boiled down to referentiality.

In order to make our point, let us return to sentences (1), (2), and (3). They are obviously substitutable as far as their propositional content is concerned.

From the point of view of speech act theory, they are equivalent in their locu-
tionary and assertive function, but they differ at least in their illocutionary
force. For the moment, though, we are only interested in their content as assertions.

(1) answers the same questions as (2) and (3), as well as other questions
that are excluded by (2) and (3). That selection process is accomplished through
the specification of interrogatives. (2), for instance, indicates which question has
been dealt with through the explicit use of an interrogative expressing that
question. Several questions, instead of a single one, could be involved, but the
presence of an explicit interrogative limits the number of possible questions
answered by the proposition. (1) and (2), for example, could be uttered in
answer to questions such as *What did Napoleon do?* or *Who was Napoleon?*,
but (1) could also be uttered in order to signify:

(8)   All dictators lose, one day or another, even apparently successful
ones.

In other words, (1) could answer *What **did** happen at Waterloo?*, whereas (2)
could not, since we have a *who-question* embedded in the clause. This *who*-
question is absent from (1). As a result, (1) does not exclude *what-questions.*

Interrogatives can be used when some meaning must be ascribed to predicates. Our argumentation also shows why predicates as well as names have a
reference and why names are the required complement to predicates and thereby
give rise to judgments. Interrogatives specify terms and indicate what they mean,
even though the question of the meaning of these terms is not directly asked.
Deleted or not, a complete sentence ensues when the interrogatives covering
each term are saturated. An interrogative is at the same time referential and
unsaturated. The question to which it always refers back is given through
another term (sometimes a sentence, but the problem of the nature of sentences
is then displaced), and the term and the interrogative together constitute a
complete entity called a sentence. Those interrogatives have a referring function,
but they are called on in order to specify meaning. Thus reference and meaning
are associated in a typical situation, though this association should not blind us
to such a degree that we grasp meaning in terms of reference, as if such an intrinsic relationship had to exist. The truth of the matter is that the more reference is specified, the more the terms involved are known and alternative readings
out-of-the question. Being so, these terms do not require interrogative clauses
to make them understood. Questioning gives meaning *and* ascribes a definite
reference, but its presence as a third and fundamental variable does not allow

us to merely equate meaning *with* reference as if this link were natural. Instead, this link is obviously due to the interference of questioning in the process of signification. At any rate, in the case of terms, e.g. names, the interrogative serves to tell us who Napoleon was by stipulating what he did at Waterloo, for instance. Interrogatives are deleted in response to the level of understanding: the more one understands what is in question, the less one needs to specify which one of many possible questions a statement answers and the more one knows what answers the terms present in the description, that is, the reference. (1) corresponds to an implicit question which is clear enough (or assumed to be so) to be left out, while (2) and (3) refer to increasingly specified possible questions, which they can answer with increasing amounts of information. The speaker supplies such specific information in cases when he has reason to believe some misunderstanding could arise. (3), for instance, could be expanded further if the addressee proved unable to understand the words employed.

The equivalence of (1), (2), and (3) lies at the core of the substitution view of meaning.[6] Our examples could easily be submitted to a Fregean analysis in terms of sense and reference. But such an analysis is only a particular case of the more general view that meaning is the link between *a* question and *an* answer. When some answer can be legitimately singled out in a given context, it reflects this relationship between questioned answers. A judgment – and this holds for texts as well since what we face here is a general feature of language – can express a solution as well as a problem. If the problematological difference is not clearly apparent to the addressee in the given context, it is always possible to render the link between question and answer, i.e. meaning, explicit. This expansion preserves what the original statement affirms by stipulating *that* it affirms *it*. This gives rise to an equivalent proposition that is called the *literal meaning* of the first judgment, because the equivalent statement is produced on the basis of an interrogative expansion of some words contained in the judgment that is being explicated. In reality, the mechanism is more general and determines the whole process of meaning explication: to relate some answer to a given question by saying *what* it answers, i.e. *what* it says, amounts to saying what it means. The literal meaning duplicates the initial statement by saying that it is an answer, i.e. by relating its assertoric content to the question it answers. That is why meaning is substitutional.

When we remark upon a given statement's status as an answer, we do not necessarily imply that we should proceed to an interrogative expansion of that statement. Otherwise, only literal meaning would be possible, and something like (8) would never make sense. A more fundamental reason lies in the fact that the answerhood of an answer does not *a priori* limit itself to an explicitation of the question in terms of the potential internal interrogatives that such an answer suggests. This procedure is but one way of exhibiting what is in question in what is said. This process is required when some sentence is singled out *and* nothing but that sentence can furnish its own meaning. The more general procedure, which includes interrogative expansion as a particular case, is the following: when we state an answer, we do not say "This is an answer", nor do we say "This is what I mean: . . ." We just state the answer, and thereby, we say *what* it says without saying *that* it says *it*.

This apocritical feature of statements implies referentiality; referentiality is a necessary consequence of the process of stating an answer since our answers, being answers, do not refer to themselves and do not stipulate their status as answers, but refer to something else which is consequently external. This is due to the requirement embodied in the problematological difference: the question is kept implicit, or at least excluded in some way from the realm of answers. Answers do not express their nature as answers but something else called the 'assertoric content'. Answers must not say what they answer, nor assert their own answerhood, because this would imply that the question they 'solve' is their assertoric content. It is not the aim of an answer to render explicit the question it 'solves', since this process would not solve it but would simply duplicate it, though now at an explicit level.

Even if the content of an answer is not its status as an answer, if the answer does not refer to itself but *must* refer to an outward reference, it is nonetheless an answer. A such, its meaning stems from what is in question, and therefore, from its nature as an answer; the link between what it says and some question which initiated the speech is the source of its meaning. The act of specifying in what respect a statement or a text is an answer does not add anything to the content of the statement or discourse. Rather, it links that content to some question. This *substitution* preserves what is said, and only *adds* to our information to the extent it answers a request for meaning. The answerhood of an answer is itself an answer although not to the same question as the original answer: the speaker is supposed to know the question to which he has responded, even if *we* do not grasp it.

The meaning of an answer stipulates why and how it is an answer, and therefore lets us know the question it solves. If an answer to the question of meaning provided by the statement's status as an answer can only be found in the sentence and nowhere else, that status as an answer must be expressed through some interrogative expansion resulting in the literal meaning of the sentence in question. As seen earlier, an answer containing an interrogative clause presents its question as resolved and indicates which particular question was in question. This indicator tells us the meaning of an answer which is equivalent from the semantical point of view to the first answer. The general procedure, however, consists in incorporating the question involved into the discourse under consideration. This amounts to showing how the discourse answers the question to which it responds. However, this procedure cannot boil down to an interrogative expansion (a) when we face a text or a discourse (which always presents itself as a unity) rather than a single sentence, or (b) when we already understand the terms of the sentence. Something other than literal meaning is then at stake, something irreducible to the problematological analysis of the components of the sentence.

An interrogative expansion is inadequate for the consideration of meaning in all its generality (c) when sentential analysis is insufficient and it becomes clear that we cannot isolate a sentence. The situations (a) and (b) are, in fact, particular cases of (c).

As a result, the analysis of meaning in terms of interrogative clauses is necessary when an individual sentence must be understood literally. The 'wh-movement' reveals the *grammatical* structure of meaning in sentences considered in isolation. The reason why that procedure rightly applies in the case of a single statement lies in the very nature of meaning: as a question-answer relationship, meaning appears literally within isolated sentences and can be disclosed through a componential analysis that reveals the question(s) dealt with and that also reveals, as a corollary, the references involved. The study of interrogative clauses should be seen as the only way to determine the question(s) treated in isolated sentences and should also lead to an emphasis on the role of such clauses in the particularization of meaning. We will go on to a more general consideration of this role in terms of the question-answer relationship. More will be said about meaning later (chapter 6), but we should make some of its aspects quite clear now. We can begin with an example borrowed from a non-linguistic sphere. In *The Third Wave*, Alvin Toffler gives us an analysis of industrialization in terms of the so-called 'Second Wave', his term for the cleavage between producers and consumers that resulted in an increased need to concentrate on rendering the market more efficient to bridge the gap between them. The birth of the factory is seen as a consequence of the principle of harmonization of specialized tasks that is inherent in large scale industrialization. Workers are gathered within factories to meet the demand for goods that had been previously manufactured by the consumers themselves. The rise and rapid extension of the market impelled individuals to specialize in some activity of production and to cease to produce mass-produced commodities they could buy more cheaply elsewhere. Some marxists object that Toffler does not *understand* the phenomenon of the factory. Whether they are right or wrong does not concern us here. We are interested in the way they formulate their criticisms in terms of the *understanding* of a phenomenon. According to them, the birth of the factory does not *mean* what Toffler says it means; he did not grasp the true *meaning* of that phenomenon. Why? The answer is simple: Toffler does not see the *problem* that factories were meant to solve, namely the exploitation of the workers meant to bring about the increased profits that necessarily result when workers are gathered together to perform complementary tasks. Toffler does not perceive the problem, because he thinks that the problem lies elsewhere, in a so-called cleavage caused by this Second Wave of progress. Since he does not perceive the real problem, Toffler does not understand the factory phenomenon and fails to explain what it really means. We are not forced to agree with the critics, but the dynamics of their criticisms is of particular relevance to what we say about meaning:

(a)   The meaning of a phenomenon is determined once we know the particular problem it answers. The knowledge of this problem results in the correct interpretation.

(b)   Someone who does not understand the phenomenon is mistaken about the problem involved. He does not see it or takes another problem to be the real problem.

This attitude which consists in associating meaning with a question-answer complex is not limited to language, but involves social phenomena as well; theorists must deal with meanings, but so must society.

Let us now return to the notion of meaning as we find it in linguistic phenomena. Our aim is to explain why we still conceive of meaning as substitutional despite our rejection of the substitution view of meaning. To put our argument in a nutshell, the substitution view does not hold, since it is based on a propositional theory of language in which propositions are the basic units to be considered, the alpha and the omega of the theory of meaning. As discussed earlier, isolated sentences do not exist. We can always consider a single sentence and derive its literal meaning, as we did with (1). In so doing, we derived (2) and (3). Sentences are given literal meanings from interrogative expansions in accordance with syntactic rules; the deletion process is governed by our knowledge of semantics. Literal meaning can be defined as the question-answer relationship that results exclusively from the structure of the sentence itself.

Our argument therefore does not go as far as to deny the existence of literal meanings. They are, in a way, abstractions since the question on which some interrogative clause is based must really have been asked. It is this pragmatic basis of interrogative expansion, however syntactical the process may seem, that deters speakers from interrogative expansion *ad nauseam.* Our contention is that we do not relate to sentences as if we *had* to restrict ourselves to their literal meaning. Our understanding of their literal meaning cannot arise from an analysis of individual sentences taken in isolation. Rather, it is the apocritical autonomy of sentences which reveales their literal meaning.

Isolated sentences do not exist. Does this mean that we never encounter single sentences in our everyday practice of language? Of course not. What we should understand by this assertion is the following: we cannot analyze language as if sentences were its units, that is, as if sentences were some kind of universal measure for what happens in linguistic practice. This simply does not work. Our argument, then, proceeds from a theoretical standpoint which, if not respected, leads to blind spots and fallacious generalizations. When do we face single sentences? When we wish to understand one sentence, we then want to get its meaning, the *literal* signification that is supplied as the answer to the possible but underlying *What do you mean by ...?* question. This answer is bound to be a substitution in the Fregean sense but for non-Fregean reasons. The inquirer breaks up the speech continuum, precisely in order to isolate some sentence *which is then reinserted into another context*, that is, into the sphere of dialogue.

Answers, once produced, acquire some autonomy with respect to the questions that elicited them. Once the questions which were meant to be resolved through resort to language have been answered, these answers emerge as mere statements or sentences. It is as though they had never been produced in response to definite problems, as if those problems had never existed. The umbilical cord is cut off. The answers can still fulfill the two fundamental functions of language: to express problems and give solutions. In other words, any answer is by itself apocritical *and* problematological. It pertains as much to the level of solutions as to that of problems. This, of course, establishes the possibility of dialogue. An answer offered as such to an addressee in response to some question of shared interest may turn into a question for him or her. For the addressee, this answer is not an answer but requires an elaboration in the form of some other answer to the initial question raised by the speaker. The speaker's statement leaves that question open insofar as his answer appears questionable to the addressee, who may go on to initiate a dialogue by *responding* to the speaker's statement. The problematological difference between questions and answers is guaranteed by the fact that what is an answer to one person may always turn out to be a question to another. All answers are apocritical *and* problematological even if, in virtue of the problematological difference, they are not so with respect to the same questions or questioning processes.

Although they are apocritical, answers, when questioned about their meaning, are expanded problematologically. In fact, it is because answers are both apocritical and problematological that they can be translated into interrogative clauses that preserve their assertorical content. Since the question asked by the interpreter of a sentence is not the same as the problem of the speaker — whose goal was not to tell the meaning of what he said but merely to say it — the sentence is problematological with respect to some question-answer link contained in the statement but not asserted as such. The interlocutor asks that this link be rendered explicit and thematic. If someone does not understand a sentence I have just uttered, for example, he is likely to *ask* me what was in question in what I said. If I answer in an irrelevant way, he will reject my answer by saying that 'it' is not the question; if, on the contrary, I want to stress that the meaning of a sentence is such and such, I will say that this or that was the question that I have dealt with. And so forth. No matter what I say, I raise a question, and deal with it in my answer;[7] the meaning of my sentence consists in its relation to the question I had in mind when I uttered it. By revealing its own status as an answer, my statement refers back to some question and designates itself as *its* answer and, at the same time, supplies its topic if it had been unknown to part of the intended audience. The addressee's problem of knowing what the speaker's question or problem was is solved by a statement stipulating in which way the speaker's sentence serves as an answer. Examples (1), (2), and (3) above illustrate this point.

Meaning can then be defined as the question-answer relationship, and emerges as an answer to some hermeneutic questioning process whose goal is to make the answerhood of statements explicit. Because of the autonomy of statements, all answers can be reinserted within new questioning processes, even though they have served as conclusions for previous ones. Answers can be turned into questions, as if they were not conclusive (apocritical) ones but rather reformulations or displacements of the problem they were meant to solve. They can be used as stepping stones in some new questioning process and can thus contribute to the resolution of this new process. In sum, answers raise questions even when they solve others. Scientists know that results can feed fresh inquiry and that a hypothesis can be considered as a kind of result. Answers are problematological in the sense that they refer to questions by answering or suggesting them. But they also repress their status as answers; they do not say they are answers and do not refer directly to the questions which they serve to answer. Answers just say *what* they have to say, and this is what I have called their apocritical feature. It is in virtue of this apocritical autonomy of answers that they refer to *something* other than themselves, namely to *what* they say. The stipulation of an interrogative clause amounts then to the stipulation of a reference; the absence or superfluousness of such a clause implies the implicit or assumed knowledge of that reference. Thus questioning, when employed in a process of inquiry into meaning, is associated with reference. Since it is apocritical, an answer refers to something other than itself, to the world and to objects. This explains why language can be defined as being made up of signs, i.e. of entities which *are* what they are precisely because they refer to what they are not. Language is forgetful of itself. Therein lies its true function, or at least the ultimate condition for fulfilling language's functions.

An answer is apocritically undistinguishable from a statement. And statements are ultimately nothing but answers. They crystallize a propositional content, also called a *truth*, as if it were self-sufficient. If a statement does not appear *as* apocritical, it also means that it does not appear as an answer. If it did, it would also be problematological since answers, in their very status as answers, expressly reveal the presence of corresponding questions. Through the suppression of its own answerhood, a statement emerges as referring back to questions which, being already resolved, are suppressed too. The dialectic of questioning shows up quite clearly here: answers, by referring back to questions, suppress these questions, but simultaneously suppress themselves as answers in virtue of their answerhood. They do not appear as answers so that only *what* they say will emerge. Apocritically, they are not answers, but mere statements referring back to questions they have solved by not having to solve them anymore, by not having anything more to do with them. Autonomy and the claim for truth result from this process that makes answers independent with respect to the originating questions. Referring back to questions which have ceased to be posed means ceasing to refer to those questions and referring to something else instead. This 'forgetfulness' of the origin of such statements leads to the requirement that they be justified in *what* they say. Truth functions as the ground for affirming what the statement says, if no other statement does it by justifying the original statement. This displaces the claim for underived truth to some primary statement.

The dialectic of questioning indicates that answers are what they are insofar as they do not refer back to the questions they refer to by virtue of their status as answers. There is no contradiction here if we recognize that a *process* of autonomization takes place. An answer is an answer insofar as it does not say it is an answer. The apocritical feature of answers lies in this process of repression. On the other hand, answers are apocritical and thereby refer back to the questions that they have solved, as well as relate to *others* in virtue of the problematological difference. They solve questions by not mentioning them. This process of repression itself is part of the solution. This explains why the dynamic aspect of language as thinking is very seldom perceived. Theorists tend to see language as 'something out there', as a fixed corpus, or as isolated sentences that can be put together. Thinking would logically take place before any linguistic item is produced. But language is thought, and thinking takes place through and in writing or speaking.

The problematological difference is undoubtedly a *topical* one in the sense that it expresses a categorial distinction. It is also a *dynamic* one. The dynamics associated with the problematological difference is a dynamics of expressive repression of the problematic at the level of answers, answers that put an end to the process or that contribute to its unfolding by being problematological. What is a problem is referred to as being suppressed at the level of reference. This is no contradiction but merely the expression of a process of displacement where what is present is only there as a question, a presence that is also an absence due to the fact that the question is presented as solved. The apocritical feature of answers takes care of the status of questions at the level of answers. The word *apocritical* means that answers do not refer to themselves, i.e. that they do not mention the questions that they solve. But answers *are* apocritical, and this also means that they do refer to these questions in some other sense. Being apocritical is therefore a problematological feature of answers in their dynamic aspect. Answers embody the problematological difference through a process that expresses questions in terms of answers and ends up on a linguistic level where there is no longer question of answers and questions. Language can then become a veil or a mirror with respect to the external world, which encompasses 'subjects' as well as 'objects'. From a dynamic point of view, an answer refers to questions; from a topical point of view, an answer only refers to what it asserts, positively or negatively. This latter possibility, on the other hand, can only be understood problematologically. The fact that there are two possible ways of asserting a statement clearly derives from the fact that any statement *is* or *is not* an answer to the question which initiated the process of language.

As a result, answers are apocritical, and therefore, they must also be problematological. But this difference, which is a difference between the questions referred to, leads to a repression of itself; and answers consequently do not appear at the level of explicit statement as answers even if from a pragmatic point of view, they are *used* and seen as such.

2.6. *Is meaning really substitutional?*

Meaning is often described in terms of substitution. This seems to be the case even in the problematological conception, as far as isolated sentences are concerned. The reasons given for this, however, differ as much as do the categories employed in a propositional theory, e.g. Frege's. Nonetheless, the proposition although conceived as an answer, seems to remain the unit of language. Isolated sentences do not exist as such in everyday scientific or literary discourse. How, then, could meaning be substitutional?

If the meaning of a text (or of a sentence) were another text (or another sentence), we could not mean what we say or write without first laying down the 'other' text (or the 'other' sentence) and so it would go on endlessly. Thus meaning is no substitute but rather is immanent in what we say and write. Meaning usually goes without saying and, as a result, understanding is often implicit: it corresponds to grasping the answerhood of what is said or written, and the answerhood is immanent in the answer itself, although in a repressed, implicit, way. The answer in question is perceived by the questioner as an answer and what is in question is therefore understood. No substitution at all is required for such an understanding to take place.

If meaning is seen as substitution, it must be in some extended sense of the word 'meaning', namely as an explicit answer to the question of meaning, i.e. when meaning resists the implicit process of discovery of what is in question in what is said or written. If the answer is a substitute for the original answer, then we might be tempted to say by extension, as many have, that meaning *itself* is substitution, when only interpretation is so. And by extension again, any reformulation of a questioned answer that, in plain words, will be called its meaning and be counted as a substitute.

This double fallacy is not entirely groundless. If A means 'B', A is equivalent to B and B can also replace A. We could write, for instance, *pass* and *do not pass* instead of using green and red traffic lights, since the latter means the former in the linguistic code. Consequently, if an interpretation that stipulates the meaning of a sentence is another equivalent sentence, the interpretation is equivalent to the meaning, and meaning and interpretation cannot be distinguished from one another. Hence the assumption that meaning is always substitutional.

This fallacy has had questionable effects upon literary theory. It leads to the idea that literary interpretation, which is textual, is like the duplication of some statement, a repetition put in other terms, a sign or a signifier, which by definition, is that which stands for or refers to something else.

> "Michael Riffaterre argues that the reader ... experimentally establishes implication of the code of the narrative by deriving repetitions and how they function. These functions make it possible for the reader to interrelate descriptions, characters, and objects, so that the work as a whole becomes a single sign ... If Riffaterre sees the novel as a sign, Brian Fitch analyses the Bataille novel as the story of word."
> (Cohen 1978: 4)

The conflation of meaning and the explication of meaning refers back to some version of the substitution view of meaning. Meaning is not fundamentally substitutional even if the process leading to it consists of substituting an answer for another, e.g. a text for another text. What is substituted cannot be characterized in terms of results but of a process. As an answer, meaning can be seen in reference to substitutionality. But the question-answer relationship never appears in the theories that conceive of meaning as substitution, because, if it did, it would reveal that meaning is not substitution, and that interpretation, as a process, is substitutional only insofar as it relates questions and answers, problematological answers and apocritical ones. As shown in note 6, sentences (1), (2), and (3) are not totally substitutable, but only insofar as they involve the same question. In themselves, (1), (2), and (3) do not necessarily answer the same, and exactly the same questions. In other words, these three sentences are not *logically* substitutable. They are substitutable only insofar as they respond to or deal with the same question.

Meaning, therefore, is not substitution. In spite of this affirmation, we shall follow tradition and continue to speak of the meaning of a sentence or a text when we talk about what is, strictly speaking, its interpretation. Substitution as the reference theory of meaning conceives of it does not exist in natural languages, but, in contrast to Quine's assertions, this does not imply that meaning is a meaningless notion. Single sentences do not exist. The truth is that we always single out a sentence or a term within the framework of a given question, within a context where it makes sense to question its meaning. The answer will be another answer which can be seen as the literal reformulation of and substitute for the original answer in question.

Meaning, then, can be assimilated to substitution, however secondary, reductive, or improper this assimilation actually is. The language of substitution stems from sentential analysis, which has been shown to be inadequate. Meaning is not substitution and is nonetheless, to some extent, substitution. The proper manner to conceive of this substitutability is to realize that it is related to understanding as questioning and to meaning as answerhood. Equivalent answers may well be non-substitutable on a logical basis and nonetheless be related to each other as meaning is to that which is meant. Substitution is problematological in the sense that sentences are substitutable with respect to a given question, or even to a given problematic. Meaning is problematological substitution, and this way of thematizing it necessarily takes care of the dynamic aspect involved in the attainment of meaning and of the repression of this dynamic. The notion of a problematological substitution involves the notion of an equivalence based on questioning and of the disappearance of question processing into a substitution which is only such as a result of the process, instead of being an equivalence *per se.* The idea of problematological substitution also accounts for the apparent contradiction between meaning as substitutional and meaning as non-substitutional. It is not substitutional in the traditional sense as we find it in the componential or reference theory of meaning, and it is nonetheless substitutional, as we all know from common sense experience, but is so in a particular way that directly involves problems and questions. Hence the need to capture this substitutability through problematological theory. In the framework of problematological theory, meaning is substitution under certain circumstances, but substitution itself is understood as a consequence of the question-answer complex in language, that is, as an *extension* (and not as the whole) of a more general view which is basically defined in constant reference to questioning.

Meaning is substitution because a statement is an answer, though in a repressed way. The passage to the explicitness of answerhood preserves the content (i.e. the reference) of the answer and simply highlights some relationship holding between that content and its formation. This can be seen from a traditional point of view, in the pragmatic procedure in which a sentence is inserted into some new setting of occurrence. Basically, the procedure substitutes for what is said or written something which still says the same thing but says it from another standpoint. Thus one supplements the information conveyed by explicitly specifying it. The hermeneutic (explicit) answer which is that of *reception* differs from the original answer in that it interprets the original from another standpoint. A speaker or an author does not specify what he/she means by *what* he/she says, he/she just says *it*. But the interpreter, if he/she is right, cannot say something other than what the speaker or author said. Meaning is then the capital bequeathed by a speaker which is essential in order for the dialogical transaction to take place.

The question that the questioner-interpreter wishes to discover in his/her hermeneutical process is the problem of the speaker or the author that gave rise to the statements whose meaning is in question. When some sentence is taken in isolation, this procedure can only result in the mention of the very question embodied within the assertion, the question solved by the statement and which, therefore, appears only as an absent presence. Hence we find the expansion of the assertion through resort to some interrogative clause explicitly specifying what was implicitly presupposed, i.e. what is at stake in the sentence and which is dealt with in it. In other words, the substitution view of meaning is the only possible conception we can have if the unit of language taken into consideration is the isolated and free-floating sentence. Compositional substitution is, in reality, the only possible way of relating an assertion to the question with which it deals, when no other element can be considered or has to be considered. But we should be attentive to the function of such substitutions: they are simply the result of a more general process which consists in relating what is explicit to the questions they treat and which, in definite situations, leads the interpreter to one equivalent assertion stipulating what *is in question* in the original assertion. The two assertions are equivalent to the extent that what is implicit in the first is rendered explicit in the second, and the assertoric content is the same. By telling what is *contained* in the first assertion, the second one is analytic with respect to the first.

We can easily generalize: substitutionality, as propositional theory sees it, is seriously restricted. It is mostly based on equi-referentiality. As a theoretical standpoint, the substitution view must be discarded. On the other hand, it is a fact that meaning is substitution; the situation in which sentences are taken into consideration is but a particular case of something more general. The meaning of a discourse is expressed through the substitution of a question for the answer as a response to another implicit or explicit questioning of the answer's meaning. The question is expressed as an answer with respect to the hermeneutic query. If the second questioner is faced with a whole discourse, the problematic raised in that discourse is not an equi-referential version of each sentence of that discourse. We shall see *what* the problematic is in the next two chapters, and *how* textual semantics functions in the last chapter.

When a single sentence is considered out of any context, or rather, since this seldom happens, when one single sentence is questioned as to what it literally means, the passage from the answer to its embodied question is solely based on the referentiality of the terms the answer contains. This gives rise to a second answer expressing the question the answer deals with, as (2) does with respect to (1). But this process is but a particular case of the substitution of one discourse for another *which more often than not is not a sentential substitution.*

2.7. *Conclusion*

In this chapter, we have developed a theory of reference and a theory of language distinct from the classical theory and thus not dependent on the propositional view of language. In spite of its far-reaching implications, the *problematological conception* puts forth minimal requirements that were already familiar to pragmatists like Dewey. We have tried to show that the unsatisfactory theories of reference, meaning, and judgment could be changed into a more adequate view which is *a priori* capable of grasping texts and discourse, as we shall soon further examine.

The substitution view of meaning has proved to be an indefensible theory. Actually, meaning is substitution only in some cases. The general situation can be described as follows: a statement is conceived in terms of its being an answer, and the process of understanding is nothing but a substitution of a question-answer relationship for a mere assertion or group of assertions. Understanding is always substitutional in this sense, but its outcome, i.e. meaning, is not *eo ipso* a literally and logically substitutional statement.

3. THE RHETORIC OF TEXTUALITY

3.1. *Textual meaning is rhetorical*

Most of the time we can understand the sentences that are addressed to us. This implies that we can infer the question(s) raised by the sentence, that is, the questions behind the sentence that are resolved by the sentence — on the basis of what is said. Is the meaning of a text or of any sustained discourse the sum or the product of the meanings of the individual sentences? Put in other terms, my question amounts to the following: is a text an entity or not? The answer is not as simple as we would like it to be.

In many cases, we grasp some meaning in a text by discovering the sense of the statements it contains. On the other hand, the text may say something other than its constituent statements. The meaning of a text is neither a mere juxta-position of statements nor one global and precise proposition summing up all the others contained in the text. To understand a text is, first of all, to have access to the meaning of the sentences composing the text. But that is surely not what we call having an understanding *of the text*. We may undoubtedly ask for the meaning of a text and mean thereby that we only want to see a stipu-lation of the meaning of *some* of its sentences, as if they were written in a foreign language, as if some words could not be understood. We should call this understanding a *request for translation*. It amounts to singling out some sen-tences from the text. It leads to the stipulation of literal meaning, as in the case of sentences such as (1).

But when we say we do not understand a text, we mean something else and we certainly do not request the interlocutor to take each sentence one by one and reformulate it in other terms. To understand a text means to understand it as *a whole*, as *a text*. As a result, it is surely not the literal readings of its sen-tences that are in question. We are rather concerned with their figurative meaning, with what we call their textuality in the work in which they occur. Textuality is the non-literal reading of a set of sentences considered as a whole, i.e. considered synthetically. Actually, most of the time we do understand the language and the words employed in a text we want to comprehend. What we mean by the meaning of a text *could not* be supplied by translating each sentence one by one into other sentences, since it is the *text*, not its constituent sentences, that is in question. The text is nothing besides those sentences but nonetheless always exceeds them. Our claim is that the relationship between texts and sentences can only be grasped adequately in terms of questioning. The textuality of a continuum of sentences is the question that is figuratively posed by the answers expressed by the individual sentences of the text to a questioner called the reader.

Obviously, *A la recherche du temps perdu* cannot be reduced to a single proposition that would express all of its meaning, nor could it be equated with the succession of anecdotes, or events that we find narrated in Proust's book. Its meaning, like a secret intention, seems to lie beyond the written words of this book, so that we are not even sure that the meaning is unique or decipherable. Hence we come to the question that has been raised by some literary critics, such as Barthes: does it make sense to speak of meaning in literature? On the one hand, we find several compatible interpretations in any literary text that do not even seem to depend upon the linguistic features of the text. On the other hand, we can see in the linguistic features of the text some unity concretized in its physical presence or its author. But it displaces the problem of the unity *of meaning*: the meaning of what the author said is not a function of what he said but rather of what he was. This last question implies a displacement of the basic difficulty of discovering why the work is not by itself the bearer of its own meaning and why it is essential to move outside of the text to seek what is supposed to be a feature of the text.

Many literary critics have abandoned the concept of meaning when confronted with this conflict between a plurality of possible interpretations and the unity of a text outside the text, the vacuous unity of textuality only created by the author's name or guaranteed by the mere physical boundaries of the text. Meaning would then rest upon these last two factors. Hence most theorists have found this conception hardly credible.

Our previous discussion of meaning will help us surmount this apparent antinomy.

(a) In many aspects, a literary text is no different from any other text. Ordinary sentences are seldom isolated in real-life situations, but rather are produced in a continuum which constitutes their physical as well as intentional unity. Hence the revealing role, from the viewpoint of psychoanalysis, for instance, of the *non sequitur* in discourse. Like spoken sentences, texts are not made up of unrelated components.

(b) A substitutional answer to a question of meaning can be made *only* if *one* sentence is in question, and indeed *should* be made if the question is directed towards the *words* composing the sentence and what they mean, as illustrated by example (1) above. Meaning is not, most of the time, a mere logical or semantical substitution. If, for example, I say:

(9)   It is one o'clock.

I may also assert that, in special circumstances, I have said *I am hungry*, or *It is time to sit down at the table.* To say *It is one o'clock* is to say these things. The word *is* indicates not an identity but a substitution authorized in virtue of context. In sum, the statement that it is one o'clock *is* — quite unlogically, but pragmatically[8] — in a particular context the affirmation of a desire to satisfy my hunger. Meaning makes a statement an answer by contextualizing this answer with reference to some question. The substitution view of meaning is false when substitutions are conceived on the sole basis of logic (Quine) or of constituted and sedimented, context-free, markers of lexical or free-existing meaning (Katz). The *being* designated by the copula marking the substitution, as in *A is B* for instance, must be understood as variable, i.e. as context-dependent. Context lets us tell that, in a given case, *It is one o'clock* means [9] 'I'm hungry. Let's have lunch' rather than 'Can you drive me to the station now?' In short, the hermeneutic process substitutes answers for statements without modifying what the answers state, because their answerhood lies not in *what* they state, but in the fact *that* they state it and, ultimately, in the possibility of stating it at all.

So, when I affirmed that I rejected the substitution view, I was not claiming that, through the hermeneutic inquiry, a statement does not become an answer. Quite the contrary, for in the process of understanding, there is a process of substitution at work even when meaning is 'evident' and when the whole hermeneutical process remains therefore implicit. The words 'substitution view of meaning' represents a label for identifying a particular view of substitution that neglects questioning because it is essentially and exclusively componential and is therefore very narrow in the kind of substitutions for which it makes allowance. It is a particular *view* of substitution and of language based on the paradigm of isolated sentences, of compositional meaning, of the role of the word *be* as a *logical constant* (I emphasize these *two* words).

Now, as discussed earlier, most of the time people understand the sentences they hear in ordinary speech as well as those they find in books and literary texts. Therefore, if we ask what an author or a speaker meant by what he/she said or wrote, if we ask for the meaning of a text, we surely do not seek answers about the meaning of particular and already understood sentences. In other words, the meaning of the *Quixote* can perfectly well remain hidden to someone who knows Spanish and gets the sense of all the sentences in all the chapters. The same holds for a spoken discourse.

Should we then regard the basic meaning of a discourse or text as the speaker's or author's *intention*, as some deeper affirmation, to be perceived outside the text, in the reader or hearer, for example?

(c) Being unable to conceive of meaning on another basis than the substitution view, we would inevitably be led to look for meaning in the author's or speaker's *intention*. Meaning would be located outside of the text, and it would become meaningless to speak of textual meanings. On the other hand, we would implicitly grant validity to the substitutionalists' claim that meaning only applies to *sentences*, thus creating an unbridgeable gap between textuality and sentential meaning, instead of proving that beyond this difference lies some unity.

(d) If meaning is a question-answer relationship, the unity of a text or of a sustained discourse must also be such a relationship. What is in question in a text should not be seen as the sum of the questions answered by the sentences of the text, for these questions cease to arise since they are continuously solved in and by the text. When we understand sentences in a text, we know the particular questions they answer. Hence, if we speak of grasping what the text says as a whole, some *other* question(s), different from those dealt with explicitly and literally in the text is (or are) at stake.

There is, then, no gap of a linguistic nature between textual meaning and sentential meaning as conceived and codified by the theorists of propositional substitution. One could object that I have developed notions that are open to doubt: the notion of the unicity of texts, of the sentential (oral or written) continuum, and hence of the continuum's meaning as an independent reality, though not *sui generis* with respect to sentential meaning.

In fact, as shown in (a) and (b) above, texts exist and speech continua do too. They present themselves as interrelated sentences, and the question of meaning that arises each time we face a text or a speech involves the nature of this interconnectedness. My point here is to draw attention to the unity of *what* is said or written: whether it is a single sentence or a whole book, each presents itself as an entity to its readers. When one asks the meaning of what is said, one presupposes such a unity by addressing its 'whatness'. If sentences are textually structured, then there must be a reason for their arrangement that can be called the author's (or speaker's) intention; without such arrangement and intention, one phrase would be sufficient to do the job of the whole text.

Intention, however, should not be retained as an explanatory concept, especially not in literature. When an author writes a literary fiction, he obviously conceals his personality by means of fictional narration. His intention, then, is precisely to mask his intention and to hide himself behind the narration of a story. What can be the use, then, of seeking the intentionality of the narrative intention when literary texts are precisely meant to signify something that the author's intentions cannot explain? In fact, not all texts are characterized by *intentional opacity*. Non-literary discourse is intentionally transparent. Since such texts reveal their authors' intentions, one is finished with analyzing when one understands what the author meant, i.e. in this case, what the text expresses. Once again, we can say that the intentionality of that intention can be dispensed with and is theoretically useless to grasp the meaning of what is said: the author's intention is textually transparent. This alternative can be summed up in the following way: either the author's intention is intentionally disguised in the text and the meaning of the text cannot be revealed through recourse to the author's concealed intention; knowledge of intention is then of no use if the text does not speak by itself. Or, on the other hand, if the author meant exactly what he said, there is no need to resort to a search for intentions to understand the text, since intentions manifest themselves in the text and in its immanent meaning. Hence intentionality is useless in accounting for textual meaning in such a case. At best, we can proceed to an analysis of intentions in the case of non-literary texts in which the author has not masked his intentions as a *complementary* procedure subordinate to the *unavoidable* textual analysis. Let us remind ourselves that Schleiermacher already expressed this when he laid down his famous *principle of complementarity*. When intentions are disguised, literary critics usually resort to the concept of 'implied author', which is a construct designed as the underlying structure of the *problematic* of texts. As we shall see later, that construct proves quite useful when we want to explain how textual dialectics functions between the 'implied author' and the 'implied reader'.

To sum up, the author's intention is either adequate to the explication of meaning but useless with reference to the text itself, or it is inadequate because it is masked by the author himself. What does Flaubert's famous saying "Madame Bovary, c'est moi" add to the comprehension of the book itself?

Thus far, our claims do not imply that the unicity of meaning corresponds to the unity if the text. Since meaning is a question-answer relationship, we could

see our query as asking how we can possibly know that there is only a single
problem from which a text *qua* answer originates. Indeed, nothing prevents us
from admitting that a whole problematic consisting of several questions
underlies some texts. When a text is composed of one sentence, the problematic
is reduced to one question as long as literal meaning only is considered.
For the time being, it suffices to keep in mind that the interpreter's attitude
towards a text is identical irrespective of whether a text addresses one or several
questions. We should be solely concerned with the distinction between the
questions debated *in* the text by its constituent phrases and the question dealt
with *by* the text as a whole. Example (9) illustrates this difference quite clearly:
what is in question *in* the text is time, but the question with which the interlocutors are confronted bears upon the speaker's wish to have lunch. The latter
question is harder to formulate with precision because it is left unspecified.

The meaning of a text transcends the literal sense attached to each of its sentences. Even if the answer refers to a plurality because meaning is plural, this
fact remains. The meaning of a text is like the implied question in (9). An implied question naturally suggests the existence of an implied questioner as well
as a reader or a listener. We can surely affirm that, though a text is composed
of sentences which are understood literally, as soon as we encounter them, the
whole text or speech behaves as a non-literal piece of language: the text as such
has no literal meaning with respect to the various sentences composing it. The
question(s) at stake in the text, dealt with *by* it, is (or are) not literally the
question(s) solved in the text through the various sentences. When we seek the
meaning of the *Quixote*, for instance, we do not mean that we do not understand the written words and the sentences contained in the book, we simply
mean that, beyond that understanding *and on the basis of it*, we require a
residual but capital piece of information, the key to the whole book as a unity.
Therefore, we do not require the literal reformulation of the sentences of the
text, but request their non-literal interpretation. Meaning is not a reformulation
of the text but appears in this situation as a non-literal answer with respect to
the various propositions embodied in the text. The text literally means what it
does not say or, in other words, does not say literally what it means. The text is,
with respect to the literal meanings provided by its sentences and questions
solved in them, figuratively a question. It requests a figurative answer *with
respect to the answers given in the text*, an answer (or several answers) that
stipulate(s) the nature of the text as an answer to this figurative question. A
text is not literally a question, but as a self-sufficient entity, it is a figurative
question. And to read means to answer this figurative question by stipulating at

least mentally which problematic is *figured out.* To figure out a problematic is to give a non-literal reading of the literal meanings found in the text. This non-literal reading is the goal of the hermeneutic investigation. We then have a literal answer to the figurative meaning of a text. A non-literal meaning is that implied by the literal meanings. Textual meaning is rhetorical. A text acts as the non-literal version of its literally interpreted components and thus behaves in a manner that is, as we shall see, essentially problematological. A text then functions like a sentence endowed with figurative meaning, i.e. with a rhetorical bearing. In (1), for instance, what is in question is Napoleon and what happened at Waterloo. But the question(s) is (or are) expressed as solved. Literal meaning is supplied by interrogative clauses which render those questions explicit. Now, let us suppose that the speaker of (1) means (8) instead of (2). First, he *also* literally means (1), because (8) could not be suggested if (2) was not priorly understood. If the meaning conveyed *by* (1) is (8), one cannot say that the question to be discovered is the one solved *in* (1). The meaning which is *given* is not the meaning that (1) *has*, since (1) has (8) as a signification. If there is a real question raised by (1), one which is not already solved, then it must be (8), among other possible ones. The same reasoning holds for (9) and its various non-literal readings.

When we search for the meaning of a text whose sentences are already understood, we are faced with the same situation: what needs to be understood is the textuality of the sentences composing the work , and not the questions literally dealt with in the sentences of the text. In other words, textual meaning cannot be considered as literal or sentential meaning, knowledge of which is presupposed, but ought to be considered as something outside the meaning of all the sentences of the text. That is what we call textuality. The fact that it transcends the sentences of the text and seems to vanish has possibly been the most convincing argument for the notion of authorial intentionality. This is so, we should add, because of the lack of an adequate theory of *textuality*. Although it transcends the sentences of the text, textuality is immanent in it. It characterizes the text as more than a combination of single sentences. The relationship between sentences that is not contained in what each sentence affirms creates that textuality.

On the other hand, even if textuality transcends the sentences of the text, it is not independent of them. The questions raised by the text, its problematic, are related to the questions dealt with in the text and its sentences. The sentences are literally comprehensible once we know the language used and the meaning of the terms employed. The text's problematic is derived non-literally.

Understanding the text *qua* text requires something else, something that can also be explained by our problematological approach, since meaning is always a question-answer relationship.

What I have said about textual meaning could remind us of the definition of literature formulated by Frye (1957: 81):

> "The literary structure is ironic because 'what it says' is always different in kind or degree from 'what it means.' In discursive writing what is said tends to approximate, ideally to become identified with, what is meant."

If we follow Frye in his definition of literature, all texts ought to be considered as literary ones. Since the question of the meaning of a text then becomes equivalent to the non-literal meaning of the question of the text, all texts should also be considered as rhetorical as well, according to the standard conception of the term *rhetoric*.

All this raises several questions. What is rhetoric? Is it different from argumentation? What do we mean by the question(s) dealt with *by* a text, and how do we discover it (or them)? Are all non-literal meanings the result of a literary enterprise? How can we spell out the difference between meaning in literature and meaning in general, or, to put it in other terms, what is the specificity of literary texts?

3.2. *Rhetoric and argumentation*

An answer is problematological as much as apocritical; though produced as if it had nothing to do with questions, it is nonetheless an answer. Insofar as it is an answer, it represses itself as an answer and refers to something else *that is says*. The answer's meaning is to be found by considering the question with which it is associated. In the case of single sentences, this amounts to expanding the answer as an answer, to specifying through an interrogative clause what is in question and what is resolved by the proposition.

Most of the time, however, texts present themselves as a unity. What is said and needs to be considered as said consists of a group of interrelated sentences. The question with which the text is associated cannot be found through the mere expansion of its constituent sentences into interrogative clauses. The problem of unity would be left unsolved; the relationship between all these questions solved in the individual sentence would still need to be considered with respect to the more general question of the meaning of the text as a whole. We have seen that the relationship between these partial questions inherent in the sentences and the question which we wish to solve, that of the meaning of the text, can be specified as the non-literal meaning implied by the partial questions. This relationship ought now to be studied in the light of its so-called rhetorical nature.

An answer has an argumentative and rhetorical impact by virtue of its problematological nature. It can express questions afresh, while it was meant to solve one specific problem. It can then duplicate that problem again if someone objects to the solution and rejects the answer *as an answer*. It can also raise and suggest other questions and lead to possible dialogues. Argumentation becomes involved if we realize that an argument is an opinion on some question which gives us a reason to think in one direction rather than in another with respect to that question. If my problem, for example, involves going out for walk, an answer affirming that the weather is fine serves as an argument (i.e. a *reason*) in favor of the decision to go out. On the other hand, this answer is not an argument *pro* or *contra* the wish to know what the weather is like: it simply gives the information on that question but does not argue in favor of anything. It is an argument only insofar as it serves as a solution to another implied question. An argument is a reason to opt for a certain answer or solution to a question or problem other than the direct question which the argument serves to answer. In other words, argumentation is a problematological notion dealing with implied questions. It relates the explicit to the implicit. The answer *John has stopped beating his wife* gives a reason to believe that John has a wife and that he used to beat her; it also provides information bearing on the question of John's present relationship with his wife; however, this answer is not an argument explaining John's behavior. It just describes his behavior. That is why a direct answer to some question that does not justify itself as an answer is groundless as an isolated statement. Its assertion is not an argument for its validity nor a justification for its being *the* answer to the question with which we are concerned. The so-called principle of sufficient reason amounts in reality to the knowledge that a given answer is the answer to a particular question, and justifies that answer's status as an answer. We then know the *reason* for its having been uttered or written. This knowledge is itself an answer to a second question which is not *directly* dealt with, i.e. the question of meaning, an answer whose specificity consists in showing that no other answer could be *the* answer to the particular question under consideration. This knowledge gives an answer to the question why the statement offered as answer is the answer and why its negation is not. Further, a direct answer to some particular question asserts a belief in what is in question in the answer, rather than in the contrary statement. But is this still argumentation? Do we face the same *question* when we consider beliefs? In fact, an answer usually does not say why it is an answer, i.e. what it *answers*. The question of its status as an answer remains a different question from the one the answer resolves, even if this question can be answered on the basis of what the answer says. This implies that the reason why we can affirm what we say is not stipulated *in* what we say, but it can nonetheless be discovered *by* what we say and the fact *that* we say it. The reason we answer the way we do is not contained in the content of what we say, but once we know why a particular statement or a text is an answer, i.e. which question has animated us to make it, we know the *reason* why we think the way we do. When two questions are at stake, as in the case of presuppositions where a second question is indirectly (implicitly) answered, in the act of directly answering the first question we have a reason or an argument located in the relationship between the two questions. Broadly speaking, this relationship delimits the field of argumentation.

Therefore, *John stopped beating his wife* is the ground for asserting *John has a wife*, as much as *The weather is fine* may be a reason to say *Let's go for a walk*. *The weather is fine* is even a reason to take that walk rather than not to take it. By itself, neither of these statements is an argument, since each directly answers a definite question and, *with respect to this question*, the statement is not an argument for thinking in one way rather than another way, including the opposite one.

Argumentation arises when, if some question is raised, some answer to this question is indirectly made, i.e. is *implied* by an answer to another question. The former answer is the *implicit* or *implied* conclusion to the latter. In (9) above, for example, *It is one o'clock* is an argument for having lunch. The statement that we should have lunch is also the non-literal meaning of (9) in a particular context. Is the discovery of meaning an argumentative process, or is it not rather the non-literal presentation of some meaning — *Let's have lunch* is a non-literal reading of (9) — which is an argumentation, an incitement to conclude something which is not said?

In sum, we shall say an argumentation exists when there is some relationship between an explicit statement or text and some implicit conclusion.

When does argumentation become rhetorical? Rhetoric has been variously characterized as a method of persuasion, as a set of tricks resorted to for the purpose of manipulating people, and as the set of stylistic devices inherent in the production of narratives. The adjective *rhetorical* is also employed to describe what is merely formal, ornamental. It is surely closer to the truth to say that the word *rhetorical* disqualifies rather than qualifies. Rhetoric is indeed all these things, but differs from argumentation *stricto sensu* in the following respect: rhetoric aims at *persuading* someone while argumentation functions independently of the possible, persuasive effects the relationship between the explicit and the implicit can have. Rhetoric, however, has often been equated with argumentation for the obvious reason that one does not resort to language without the intention of convincing the addressee of what one says. The reader is often left to infer the conclusion which is not necessarily ready-made to be acquiesced to or disagreed with. Persuasion, then, is argumentatively conditioned.

In spite of this distinction, the two notions of rhetoric and argumentation have often been conflated: by swallowing the mechanisms of argumentative reasoning, rhetoric has become a very imprecise concept. We shall consider the consequences of this amalgam in a while. It is important to note, with Chaïm Perelman, that the concept of rhetoric as manipulation (Plato) or as a bundle of tropes emphasizes what are, in fact, *derived* and particular *uses* of rhetoric. Perelman and Olbrechts-Tyteca (1969: 4) define rhetoric more generally as "the discursive techniques allowing us *to induce or to increase the mind's adherence to the theses presented for its assent*." Is literature convincing? At any rate, the French structuralists have associated it with rhetoric, restricting rhetoric to literary devices and taking an argumentative reality for a rhetorical one. It is true that implicit ideas are embodied in the explicit level of literary texts, but this is argumentation rather than rhetoric. It is interesting to linger over the reasons for this confusion between argumentation and rhetoric.

This confusion is probably due to the French classical legacy, that, at least theoretically, has its origin in the Roman conceptualization of eloquence.

If we consider style as an ornamental element — to the variety of ornaments corresponds an equivalent multiplicity of stylistic figures — adopted to convey some underlying and hidden truth that *could* be put in plain terms but should not for reasons of aristocratic *bienséance* or political prudence, then it is fairly obvious that literature is rhetorical. Stylistic figures inherent in the writing of literary texts make literature essentially rhetorical: they are used to please, like *bon mots*, or to persuade.

However, this view of literary language and its corresponding forms neglects the fact that the characteristics of literature it identifies as rhetorical could legitimately be shown to be present in any discourse. In real-life situations, the choice of a form of expression is guided by similar rhetorical considerations. After all, who does not want to persuade or please his or her audience?

Rhetoric, then, gained a broader meaning than that implied by mere ornamental considerations. Rhetoric was used to attest to the presence of a figurative meaning in some piece of language, a presence that was implied by literal or grammatical structures. The literary tropes play a rhetorical role to the extent that they refer to some implicit message that they each *formulate* in their own way. Quite evidently, this modifies our understanding of the purpose of tropes, which now have nothing to do anymore with courtly usages, outside of sharing common modes of functioning. Tropes are still conceived of in terms of literal substitutes for something which is intended figuratively or, conversely, from the critic's point of view, as figurative substitutes for something which can be translated into plain language.

Now, thanks to theorists like Paul de Man and Paul Ricoeur, we know that tropes are no substitutes for literal readings. In the case of metaphors, for example, we cannot conceive of literal meaning and figurative meaning as related in such a way that the figurative can be substituted for the literal. We are *asked* to pass from one to the other, but they do not stand for each other as if we could do without one of them: metaphors *create* their own meaning, and it is only when some definite interpretation has been ascribed to them that they *die* as metaphors, becoming figures for some already constituted readings (cf. Ricoeur 1975: 141). In the case of questions, the same reasoning applies: the grammatical structure, in poetry for instance, does not always enable us to tell whether a question is rhetorical or epistemic, leaving room for different, if not contradictory, interpretations of what the reader is asked to conclude (cf. de Man 1979). Where, then, should we find the literal, grammatical, and underlying meaning or message which can be formulated in plain, ordinary, and non-literary speech?

Rhetoric was a term invented to differentiate literary language from other types of discourse, but unfortunately it failed to explain this difference since (a) everybody wants to persuade or please, and (b) the opposition of literal to non-literal meaning is a mysterious relationship, mysterious at least for our so-called rhetoricians of literature. Their attitude is due to the fact that they did not analyze the mechanisms of this relationship, which is precisely what I call an argumentative link. We shall see that if we maintain the distinction between fiction and realistic language as a linguistic difference, as the theory of literary tropes suggests, we incur the risk of not understanding how language *and literature* function.

Rhetoric is clearly the counterpart of argumentation. The rhetorical dimension can be defined as the impact a discourse has on the beliefs of an audience. To influence others, to manipulate them, to seduce them, to suggest that they conclude something, all this has to do with rhetoric. How does it happen? Argumentation tells us: a discourse is argumentative if it *implies* some conclusion, *of* a question or leading *to* another question; whether or not the audience believes the conclusion implied, there is a mechanism by which language conveys such an implication. The rhetorical impact is the other side of the coin, and we can reasonably suppose that the purpose of argumentation is rhetorical: argumentation aims at putting forth ideas in order to affect the addressee in some way.

Because of the traditional conflation of rhetoric and argumentation, we will from now on speak indifferently of rhetoric as argumentation. Our reservations have been made, and the reader will make the differentiation if and when he or she thinks it useful.

3.3. *Why should rhetoric (argumentation) be problematologically conceptualized?*

Argumentation is non-formal reasoning; that is, it provides an answer *to* some question *and thereby* suggests an answer *for* another question. Formal reasoning would exclude the possibility of alternative answers; non-formal reasoning does not exclude the implication of that alternative, on the basis of the first answer given. A question that is answered argumentatively (rhetorically) could be answered in another way, and it is further rhetorical in that it does not bluntly lay the conclusions on the table and avoids direct adverse reactions from the audience.[10] Argumentation, then, suggests a conclusion which could possibly be called into question; this explains why it is merely suggested as an answer by the *first* answer. The answer-conclusion is evoked or implied as a conclusion of an inference which is left to the addressee. By inferring the conclusion, the addressee may perhaps feel that he has reached an answer to his own problematic. The answer may seem to be a personal conclusion and hence be easily accepted by the addressee.

My point here is that argumentation gives a reason to adopt one answer among several possible ones *to* a question that can always be raised afresh since there is no single necessary answer to it.[11] Argumentation (rhetoric) has to be conceived within the framework of the question view of language. Even if arguments are rhetorically laden, we should nonetheless keep in mind our theoretical distinction between argumentation and rhetoric in order to acquire a more precise understanding of the nature of language as well as, more specifically, of literature.

Argumentation is non-formal reasoning; it provides an answer *to* some question and thereby suggests an answer for another question. The link is non-formal in that the question answered argumentatively could also be answered in another way. The negation of the answer which is suggested is therefore possible. It is the task of argumentation to present reasons for accepting such a particular answer.

Language serves as much to solve problems as to express them, to tell what some solution is as to tell what the problem was. Therefore, what is said or written raises questions as much as it answers them. Question raising can occur in two ways: formally or contextually. In the first case, the answer is explicitly put forth as a question to the addressee, though this is not necessarily accomplished by using an interrogative form.

The answer can contain explicit markers which are introduced to require a response from the addressee. These *rhetorical intensifiers*[12] belong to the 'surface structure' of what is said or written; they do not have to be followed by question marks, but they can be. It is obvious that

(10)   Is he not dishonest?

is phrased in terms that require the interlocutor to answer, to conclude that the person in question is dishonest. The speaker does not want to be *responsible* for such an accusation, so he does not say it explicitly or bluntly. Maybe the proposition *He is dishonest* would be too debatable to be directly affirmed; hence the speaker suggests a choice, an answer, to the question raised in (10) by posing another question that is meant to lead the addressee to infer that the person in question is really dishonest. The *question is rhetorical* in the sense that it suggests its own answer though, literally, it could be taken as a real epistemic request. In fact, (10) is *literally* a question, though *figuratively* it is an answer, that is, a statement. The question *implies* a statement, a conclusion which the interlocutor has to draw for himself. The advantages of such a method of question raising is that (a) it requests the addressee to take a stand in regard to the question put to him or her, (b) it enables the speaker to elude the responsibility for having said something which could have (negative) consequences for him or her, and (c) it leaves room for the denial of the implied conclusion. The question mark here acts as a rhetorical intensifier.

What is the mechanism through which this formal technique operates? This question is of importance because we face it in the study of all the other types of argumentation (rhetoric).

We have an answer which literally solves a question, and, in (10) above, the answer is problematological. The answer therefore has a definite propositional content and says something quite literally, though in (10) this is done implicitly; the speaker in (10) wishes his interlocutor to let him know whether or not X is dishonest, as the speaker believes him to be. *But*, in so doing, the speaker raises another question which is figuratively implied by what is literally said, embedded in what is said, so to speak. In other words, *by* answering a definite question or problem, a statement raises another question which, in fact, *it also answers*. Two *meanings* are then associated with the very same piece of language since two question-answer relationships arise. We can say that the first meaning is the *literal* one, and that the second, its corollary, is the *figurative* one, or vice versa if one prefers to say that there is a hidden pre-existent assertion 'behind' the discourse. Clearly, there is something 'behind' the way both meanings are embedded in one another. We can call that an *implicature* if we want to insist on the non-formal aspect of the link between literal and figurative meaning, or better an *inference* if we do not want to restrict ourselves to conversational analysis and rather want to maintain a sufficient level of generality. We can also call it an *implication*, if we are not afraid of leaving to the reader the task of going beyond the preestablished jargon to look for a common reality. The relationship between literal and figurative meaning is not substitutional in the sense that the former would *mean* the latter by translating it into plain language. Rhetoric, when equated with argumentation, is not ornamental discursivity. Figurative language adds something which is literally untranslatable. What is literal with respect to figurative language is the answer raised as a possibility by the problem represented by figurative language. This answer is a literal expression of what is non-literally said: it is equivalent in some sense, but, *ex hypothesi*, it cannot be literally equivalent nor substitutable.

The identifying feature of argumentation is that it contains a request addressed to the audience to make a move that the author does not want to or cannot directly make himself. He leaves that move to his audience with the result that its meaning is left implicit, although it is implied in the explicit. Since the supplied answer presents itself as a question, it is not taken as *the* answer to the question under consideration. The addressee is then explicitly *asked* to respond to what is said and to look for another answer which answers to the question under consideration. This second answer refers back to a second question which is not what is literally in question in the first answer. This second question is not the real expression of the speaker's problem, since his answer, though dealing with the original question *by answering it*, is not a final answer but only a step towards it. What, then, is the real question corresponding to the implied answer? Once the implied answer has been found, the addressee knows the correlated question and hence the real (figural, intended) meaning of what was said. And conversely, once the real problem that gave rise to an assertion has been discovered, the interpreter knows exactly what the author meant, i.e. what was the meaning of what he said or wrote.

The first answer is meant to make the inference of the second possible. The intentions of the speaker do not have to be independently interrogated in order to be discovered. Literal meaning is *explicitly* developed to evoke non-literal meaning; hence what a statement really means is what it does not say but rather suggests. Irony is possible as the most extreme tension between what is meant and what is said.

The second manner in which arguments are put forward does not differ greatly from the first, at least as far as the question-answer mechanism described above is concerned. The literal meaning of a sentence is understood in terms of the question it deals with: literal meaning relates the sentence to the single question it answers But once the sentence has been produced to provide a solution to a specific question, it acquires autonomy with respect to that question. The sentence can become a question again. In fact, for some person other than the one who has answered it, the sentence *poses* a question. He or she may answer by confirming or assenting to the original answer. In this case, the answer questioned by the addressee is confirmed as an answer to the original question that had been raised. As a result, even if an answer is not *literally* a question, it is one in relation to its context. Intentionally or not. In (9), a non-literal answer is suggested intentionally. Here, as elsewhere, intention neither explains nor provides meaning, though it can shed some light on it. It is through the contextual — hence objective — information that the addressee is able to discover, behind (9), the derived and implicit meaning *Let's have lunch,* and the intention of conveying it. The context enables the addressee to make the inference *Let's have lunch* from statement (9).

In general, a sentence or any other form of discourse generates questions regardless of its phrasing, even when the statement or discourse was not necessarily meant to have such an effect. The context indicates which questions are to be answered, and by context we mean the situation in which the listener or reader encounters sentences, or more specifically, the information on which the protagonists rely and that they attribute, correctly or not, to their partner, known or unknown.

3.4. *Literary versus non-literary discourse*

The two argumentative procedures discussed above are basically the same, since both procedures (seem to) provide answers to specific questions; in neither case can the meaning of these answers be explicated in terms of the specific questions they appear to answer; rather, more primary questions are implied in a discourse involving either of these argumentative techniques. The two techniques differ in their method of provoking a reaction in the addressee according to whether their primary appeal is to context or to form. Tropes, for instance, are no substitute for a figurative meaning, but literally *call for* such a meaning by literally figuring it. Metaphors are even more striking: literally, they are meaningless or recondite, so one must assume they have another significance. Literal meaning cannot be the true meaning, the valid meaning, the ultimate meaning — you name it — of metaphors, for metaphors have none. According to Aristotle, metaphors are enigmas in terms of literal interpretation. Formally, they are questions or problematological answers *ab initio* and they call for an interpretation. It is little wonder, then, that we cannot associate a second statement with metaphors which would express the original and literal meaning of the metaphorical statement, since there is no such meaning, unless they have already become *culturally fixed* stereotypes. As Ricoeur (1975: 111ff.) pointed out, the substitution view utterly fails in the case of metaphors. However, *understanding* is a substitution process, and it is no wonder that either any interpretation of a metaphor suppresses the metaphor or rather resolves it. Ricoeur failed to see that interpretation is substitutional because he did not describe the process by which language is interpreted. This process is one of questioning, and as such, leads to an answer. Metaphors are formally interrogative: their very literal formulation calls for an answer. The striking point in the description of the process of interpretation in terms of questioning holds for the interpretation of all arguments and for rhetorical discourse in general. The question-answer relationship is not defined by a substitution of an answer for the question it solves. The problematological difference, which conditions the very possibility of questioning and defines it, precludes perceiving its apocritical duplication in answer to some question, as if formulating the solution to some problem consisted merely in telling what the problem was. On the other hand, some substitution process does take place in interpretation, and opponents of Ricoeur's view of metaphor have made a valuable point in stressing the role of substitution in metaphorical discourse.

Metaphors, being literally meaningless, are formally rhetorical. Most of the time, however, there is no such thing as rhetorical discourse *per se*. If there were, it would be wonderful because we would then be able to draw a sharp line between literature and non-literary discourse: we could say, as certain French theorists do now, that non-literary discourse was non-rhetorical. These theorists beg the question by restricting rhetorical effects to the literary ones. They also assume that the presence of specific figures make texts rhetorical and that these figures are used in literature only. Example (10) above shows it clearly. After all, (10) is not in itself a rhetorical question, but can we consider (9) in itself? Example (9) may turn out to be a real epistemic question though it manifests a certain prejudice on the part of the questioner. De Man (1979) has developed that idea much better than I ever could. Yeats's "Among schoolchildren", which de Man analyzes, ends with a question ("How can we know the dancer from the dance?"), which can be understood literally as well as figuratively, but it is hard to decide which reading should be selected since the question is in itself both literal and figurative, apocritical and problematological, final and preliminary. I would like to conclude that any discourse can be rhetorical, but being rhetorical does not make it literary.

> "And although it would perhaps be somewhat remote from common usage, I would not hesitate to equate the rhetorical potentiality of language with literature itself." (de Man 1979: 129-130)

Unless, of course, one believes that the difference between literature and non-literature is not a matter of language. Anything can be subject to literary appropriation, everything that can be expressed in ordinary language can also be rendered literarily. Literature can speak of everything and of anything. And, in fact, it does.

Now, having discussed how argumentation functions according to the question view, we have to examine how texts are rhetorical in virtue of their very textuality.

A reader or a listener can always spot a figurative and derived (or implied) meaning where the author or the speaker has not meant it, simply because language lends itself to such a possibility. The case of texts is much more characteristic: *a text asks the reader to see its meaning*, it calls for some understanding of itself *as a whole, as a unity*. In doing this, texts are just like all that is said or written; specifically, they are like sentences, discourses, and speeches. Texts differ in that they are not single sentences but integrated groups of sentences. In fact, it is not true that each sentence requires a non-literal interpretation; the sentences that make up a text may even be all quite literally meaningful and nothing more, i.e. merely directly meaningful. But the text that comprises them all transcends its components by the unity of their presentation. The question the text addresses to the reader is not to be found in some particular constituent of the text, in its sentences, but in the textual unity which relates the sentences to each other. The context of each sentence is provided by all the others. Hence the text forms a circle (Heidegger) and the whole of the text can only be grasped through a *to-and-fro movement* (Spitzer). Sentences form a sequence to be discovered through successive reading. Only then can the problem the text addresses be grasped. The so-called *Erzählzeit* is the time of the resolution of this problem. The text, like the speech continuum, must be completely experienced in its development for the reader to understand the problem dealt with *by* the text. The various questions dealt with *in* the text must also be understood, though, of course, they also relate to the textual unity.

A possible objection that could be raised against this view of how one understands texts is that texts do not necessarily have to be understood globally as expressing an answer which emerges as a response to the textual unity. Can textual entities not be understood as adding partial meanings in a progressive, but non-circular succession? In fact, we proceed in such a manner when we read a text for the first time, and we rely pragmatically – in all the senses of the word – on what we know and believe and on what the sentences literally and individually say; we do not look then for a global implied meaning. But this process leads us to an understanding of only what was literally said: we see a problem resolving itself into a story with a conclusion ending it. *Erzählzeit* also means the presence of a beginning and an end. This first additive level of understanding is, as discussed earlier, necessary to reach the level of a global comprehension of the text, though the reader or listener can often stop at this level, without going 'back on his/her steps', so to speak. A story, a fictional text or a narrative, relies on the process of additive understanding to enmesh the reader in its network of beliefs and references. If the reader would *reflect* upon these, he would renounce to his 'willing suspension of disbelief' by extricating himself from this network, by going 'behind' or 'beyond' the story. It is always possible to remain at that first level due to the immanent coherence that this reading provides: secondary meaning is not sought 'behind' what is literally said, unless what is literally said proves to be a *formal* call for a non-literal reinterpretation. My contention is that, even on this first level of reading, the reader grasps some global comprehension of the text, *implied* in his piece by piece discovery of the text. He perceives at least a glimpse of the textual meaning because, as I will show later, there is an *ideological causality* at work in reading or listening. *Ideological* is to be understood in the two senses of the word: in Destutt de Tracy's sense (*une idée*) and in the modern sense in which it is related to *norms*. The second level of understanding consists of rendering explicit the idea(s), i.e. of providing an *interpretation* of the idea(s) that reveal(s) the unity of the text when it is (they are) fully articulated. To put all this in a nutshell: in all circumstances, texts have a *rhetorical* effect in the sense that they implicitly convey some belief. Though it may or may not be perceived (depending on the level of understanding employed), this rhetorical effect is nonetheless involved in the additive process of reading the text. 'Bad' literature is ideologically functional too.

As far as literary discourse is concerned, there is no linguistic difference of nature between literary texts and non-literary ones *when we consider their rhetorical effect.* As a result, fictional discourse can generate the illusion of being veridical, i.e. the illusion of mimesis.

3.5. *What is literature?*

Literary works are textually rhetorical, like all other texts. Though we know what is in question in what we hear or read, the very fact that what is said or written is expressed the way it is indicates that other questions are at stake. When we speak of discovering the meaning of a text, we are concerned with the textual arrangement of the specific sentences composing the text and with the question why the sentences are organized the way they are. This question is literally implied by the specific questions dealt with in the text; it is the key to understanding their arranged literality. We could also say that the text is figuratively asking this question about the rationale behind its organization: we can figure out what is literally in question from what is said and what is said is non-literal with respect to what is to be figured out.

In this sense, there is no rhetorical textuality which does not rely on the text's form of presentation to imply what it means. The difference between literary and non-literary texts does not depend on the presence of rhetorical effect in some texts, for, on the contrary, rhetorical effect is to be found in all texts; instead, literary and non-literary texts differ in the manner through which they attain this rhetorical effect. Hence the temptation to set up a classification of literary genres in order to categorize the variety of ways of achieving rhetorical effect. We have several competing classification systems at our disposal, all of which have proved defective. The common feature in the various literary modes of speech is *style.*[13] Style makes literary works literary and conveys the sought-after rhetorical effect. We could say that style is necessary in order to give pleasure to the reader; it encapsulates him within the problematic in the discourse, thereby developing the much sought-after fascination on the reader's part, which lies at the core of the credibility of fiction.

All this is undoubtedly true, but not fundamental. Style is the means by which literary discourse comes into being since the text must supply the information that is normally left unsaid in the normal context of speech production and reception. Literary works are literary because they have to furnish their own context of information to their unknown readers, whereas administrative reports, or oral conversations generally rely on some specific body of tacit knowledge inherent in the context of interaction between the 'author' and his audience. That is why literary discourse is *fictional*; it is unrealistic with respect to the usual situations in which we employ language. It is fictional in the sense that it must provide elements which are ordinarily implicit in the context of language use. By being unrealistic, literary discourse endangers the credibility of the information it provides, that is, it endangers its own credibility. Discourse becomes literature when the necessity arises to say something which is not habitually said when we use language to refer to the real world. One possible side effect of literature's creation of its own context is a distancing of the reader that, in extreme cases, may cause the reader to stop reading. To counter such alienation of the reader, literary texts must create some illusion, especially if they contain a narration of implicit and untold elements. Poetry, perhaps does not have to proceed this way, but novels often do. Actually, even poetry speaks of what one ordinarily keeps to oneself and thus, to an extent, leaves things implicit. Poetry has to create an environment of explicitness, which it does, for example, by provoking the reader through the use of specific formal arrangements. The reader finds himself suddenly in question, accepting (or not), liking (or not), the answers thus submitted to his spheres of explicit attention. At any rate, style is needed to render this information plausible and even pleasurable and to prevent the reader from losing interest. As a specific literary mode of discourse, poetry is characterized by its deliberate sacrifice of contextual plausibility in its approach to the problem which is rhetorically raised by its textuality. Forms, or simply, arrangement, then play a greater role than in prose, where, in contrast, we see at work a plausible explicitation of what is contextually known in everyday situations, in view of increasing the work's verisimilitude and making the context in which it presents information more adequate to the real world. In prose, form is subsidiary to that requirement. In other words, poetry is rhetorically related to the problems it expresses in a different way from prose: above all, it is characterized by an increased emphasis on formal, rhetorical procedures, such as the generalized use of tropes.

As described, the rhetorical effect inherent in textual entities can be achieved through auto-contextualization. But texts can also be formally rhetorical: they can be explicitly produced so as to be enigmatic to the reader in terms of mere form. The text is formulated in such a specific way that it presents its ideas and information literarily; ordinary textual arrangements are used and they avoid raising enigmas for the reader to solve, but instead clearly communicate and share solutions to the problems in question. Sometimes, the reverse situation is the case. Then, the literary text does not have to create illusion or generate credibility to raise and deal with the problem it is concerned with. Poetry, in general, and esoteric prose are good examples of this. In such texts, the question of meaning, including that of emotional and subjective meaning, inevitably arises, and it is in order to provoke such a question that they are formulated the way they are, leaving the reader to supplement, supply, or project his vision.[14]

In sum, when rhetorical effects are not explicitly formalized, then texts must auto-contextualize these effects; in both cases, we speak of literary discourse. In both cases, the text closes in upon itself and it becomes absolutely necessary that the reader be captured in the world or context the text creates. The text requires the reader to forget his own problems and thus enables him to get totally involved in his reading. However, the reader continues to unconsciously seek a solution to the problem of the textual arrangement while understanding its message. Hence the pleasure taken in reading. The non-reflexive level of reading is precisely a questioning process in which one brackets one's own problems while remaining on the track of their solution. Texts, however, can only bring solutions on some imaginary plane, since one cannot abandon one's real-life problems.

The reader is captured by the presentation of some problematic, and, of course, the secret of success lies in that presentation. One way of achieving it is by unfolding that problematic. Problems can be explicitly and non-rhetorically set forth as problems, as they are in detective stories. In such fiction, the so-called 'willing suspension of disbelief' is achieved through a particular literary, i.e. linguistic, arrangement which causes the reader to wish to see the problem the text presents solved. Novels create their own environment by presenting a definite problematic, and one good means of auto-contextualizing it is setting up a mystery. This method of staging such a problematic leads readers to enter into the space of the fiction, provisionally bracketing their own problems. Like spectators, they remain off the stage, providing the spectacle's audience. Literature brings a fictional, i.e. imaginary, resolution to the reader's problem. From the author's point of view, fiction is the textual presentation of that which is contextual in *real*-life situations. From the reader's point of view, fiction offers discursive solutions to non-discursive problems. This does not imply that literature provides answers to pre-existent questions of the readers, but simply that it raises questions that lead the reader to forget his own problems or to ask *himself* questions he would not have asked otherwise, and so on. In other words, the reader is asked to formulate his own answers. Hence a relationship exists between the reader's own problems, and the answers the reader comes up with to problems presented in the text. We should note that the symbolic nature of literature as dealing with those personal problems enables the reader to face his problems in a way not destructive to his ego.

In literature, especially in novels, when we have a problem, identified with the rhetorical nature of textuality, auto-contextualization means that we find the resolution as well. A narrative has a beginning and an end in relationship to the problems to be solved and the problems' solution that a literary work presents. Narration is necessarily temporal, even though there may be a tension between the chronological progression from past to present of the story's events and a narrative sequence that violates such a simple chronological unfolding; such conflicts between the sequence in which events are narrated and the sequence from past to present can be discussed in terms of *Erzählzeit* and *erzählte Zeit* (literary works employing flashback narration, such as Faulkner's "A rose for Emily", provide an example of this tension between chronological and narrative sequence). *Erzählzeit* versus *erzählte Zeit* aims at reinforcing a literary work's rhetorical effect, i.e. the problematological impact of the text which calls for a second-level interpretation. The discrepancy between the narrative and chronological development of a story's events raises problems; the reader questions what is going on in the story or the fiction.[15] This is a stylistic device, i.e. a literary procedure, that we find in many novels of this century.

But the case of popular novels is very interesting too. They do not seem to involve what I call *second-level reading* (or interpretation). Popular novels are generally associated with what is called 'escapist' or even 'bad' literature, possibly on the grounds that the unfolding of the resolution coincides with that of the problematic as if the two were one and the same. The problematic is blatantly and explicitly put forth, rendering any second-level reading superfluous. Once read, these books seem transparent. The problems they present are not put rhetorically. No reflexive process constitutive of the second-level reading, called

interpretation, need take place for the reader to be able to grasp what is meant
by the book. The process of understanding the problematic is reduced to a
mere *progressive* reading and ends with the final line of the text: then, you
have understood the book. Perhaps there was nothing to understand. It is
simply a question of following the author on the path of the story. The text as
a whole does not raise any further questions about its nature. On the other hand,
for texts requiring a second-level reading to be grasped *as a whole*, the regres-
sive procedure characteristic of such a reading must be involved, i.e., the *hermeneutical circle* or the to-and-fro movement to which I referred before. For such a
process to take place, one must be led back on one's own steps; something in
the text renders a progressive reading of the story insufficient for the reader to
comprehend the text. The literary work remains problematic because the problems
involved in the textuality of the text are not all explicitly stated; instead, many
are merely implied. On the other hand, the problems that are explicitly presented
to be explicitly solved in the text do not raise the question of the meaning of the
text, which is entirely unfolded in order to present such a resolution. The text
of a popular novel means exactly what it says and nothing more. There is no
idea beyond the narrative, unless *this* is the idea beyond it: do not ask questions
because the narrative asks and answers all the relevant questions, and beyond
these, there are none. A whole philosophy of life, after all, that makes life
simple. The writer captures the reader's attention by inducing him to follow the
development of the resolution of the questions in the text as if the problems
treated had become his own problems. Detective stories are typical of such
efforts to involve the reader. The secret of popular literature resides in its nature
as being entirely and explicitly closed in the progressive reading. A circular
procedure, i.e. a process of reflection upon the text, is then totally superfluous.
Comprehension is successive and keeps growing the further one reads. The end
of the text is the literal and conclusive answer the work provides to the question it has raised. The unfolding of the problems totally coincides with their
progressive resolution, and there are no further questions to be asked and solved
by the text's very textuality. The questions involved are solved progressively
in the text and by the text, thus rendering a global view of the text and its
problems quite senseless; such a view would add nothing to the information
previously gained in a first reading.

I would now like to stress a point concerning referentiality. Here too,
symbolic logic and the philosophy of language of the past have left their marks
on our way of describing literature. Indeed, the great influence of theories about
the analysis of language was one of the reasons I began my book by discussing

Frege's ideas. The weight of tradition is sometimes quite heavy. For example, we speak of implicature (Grice) when we should use the term 'implication', because we wrongly think that implication refers to a logico-formal inference in which all the premises are stipulated for deductive purposes. Is it not strange to see philosophers of natural language so infatuated with that particular form of language called logic that they consider natural language in terms of deviations from logical concepts, such as that of implication? For me, an 'implicature' is an implication, and just as the logical one, it connects at least two propositions: the manner in which one proceeds to derive a conclusion in logical and natural language differ in the two cases, but the goal of reaching a conclusion is the same and can be characterized as an inference.

The same criticism holds for referentiality. But there, the consequences are more damaging. One often reads that the difference between fictional and non-fictional discourse is a question of referentiality. This legacy of the Fregean analysis has led several authors to coin terms like 'pseudo-referentiality' or 'auto-referential' (cf. Stierle 1980). They seem to think that some sentences and some terms have reference, while others in the so-called fictional mode of speech do not. Not only does this beg the question of fictionality, but it also does not make sense. What we have here is an obvious manifestation of philosophical ignorance among literary critics. Referentiality falls *a priori* within language (Wittgenstein): it is an essential feature of language that it refers to something other than itself. Signs are not mere spots on paper, but rather mean *something* by indicating *it*. The whole question is *how* words refer, but the fact that they *do* refer is not in question. References, on the other hand, are *a priori* that which falls outside of language; they make the 'real world' real, so to speak, that is, they make it non-linguistic. As a result, if someone writes about somebody else's action, it is no less referential in a fiction than if the action is described in a police report. All discourses are referential by virtue of the nature of language. Hence the possibility of generating illusion arises. Fictional discourse is referential because it also speaks of things, events, and persons, though nothing in reality corresponds exactly to these descriptions. However, referentiality is not a function of the type of discourse employed, since we cannot tell from the mode of speech employed whether a scientific report is accurate or whether given sentences are veridical. What should be quite clear in this matter is that the denoted entities, i.e. the referents, are never to be found in discourse and that, as a result, the fictionality of a discourse cannot be determined from a consideration of the discourse alone; it cannot contain its references. Hence it is misleading to speak of referential discourse, because such a term falsely suggests that language could exist without the property of referentiality. *Reference* can never be found within language, since it represents things, whereas *referentiality* is inscribed within its very texture. If a discourse is imaginary, it does not mean that it has stopped to be referential. How could fictional illusion arise at all if such a withdrawal from reality were possible at all?

The question 'What is literature?' leads to another query, namely 'Why is there literature?' We have seen how literature functions literarily, but this does not explain why a discourse is arranged in a,literary manner. In other words, why does one resort to the specific rhetorical procedure called literature? Why do some rhetorical effects have to be produced literarily to be fully effective?

The answer to these questions lies in the nature of ideology. Ideology can be described as a specific rhetorical procedure which necessitates literature, either as a means to support its claims or, on the contrary, as a way to undermine it: the rhetoricalness of literature, or its rhetoricity, lies in its bearing on ideology. Literature is the fulfillment of ideological rhetoricity.

4. IDEAS AND IDEOLOGY

4.1. *The nature of ideas*

More and more, literature is considered as being rooted in ideology. But the relationship between ideology and literature is far from clear. To understand the nature of literature we must investigate the nature of ideology. Ideology is generally conceived of in political terms. Ideology is a body of ideas developed for a specific purpose: the legitimation or undermining of a socio-political order. The overall function and nature of ideas is then overlooked and subordinated to this derivative use. Where do ideas come from? Or, more fundamentally: What are ideas? How do ideas become ideology in this political sense? In order to understand how literature is related to ideology, it is important to see how literature brings ideas into play in a very general way. We sense that, in spite of its ideological basis, literature is not a mere ideological discourse or propaganda. On the other hand, we also realize that some of the ideas present in literature are ideological in the specific political sense of the term. This ambivalence in the nature of literature can be understood only in terms of an analysis of ideas in general *and* of the way literature reveals and conceals them. By restricting ourselves to a study of the connection between political thought systems and literary themes, we would fail to grasp the fundamental mechanisms of ideologization; no matter how well chosen manifestations of ideology in political and literary terms are, they still presuppose the mechanisms by which ideologies, let alone non-political ideas, are created rather than they explain these mechanisms.

To avoid this problem and to directly investigate these mechanisms, I suggest that we define *ideology* as any set of related ideas, political or not. As we shall see, there is a logic of ideology which does not depend on the material role played by those ideas, a logic which is instantiated *sui generis* by political ideologies. Basically, an *idea* is the universal manifested[16] in the particular. It appears[16] *as* particular. The particular *phenomenalizes*[16] the idea and manifests it at the empirical level. Ideas, then, enable *us*[17] to *see*[18] particular things and to *conceive* them in terms of *what* we see. Ideas and whatness are co-extensive. *What* we see only makes sense in terms of the ideas which underlie our vision. Such conceptualization gives rise to judgments. Ideas enable us to *see*, i.e. to have a theoretical grasp of objects perceived through sensory means. An idea is something general that is *in question* in something perceived through the senses, i.e. a particular. The relationship is one of subsumption, and this, as a reading of Aristotle and Kant shows, is the basis of inference. Ideas are what is seen *in* what is seen. The difference between the 'vision' of the general in the particular and the vision of the particular itself can be logically defined as being the distinction between principle and consequence. A principle is something beyond which our mind cannot go; it is a stopping point. Even if a principle is in question in a particular instance, its validity is not questioned *by* the particular. Rather, the principle serves to reveal the nature of what is seen *as* being particular . Far from being challenged by the particular, the principle or universal enables us to solve the questions raised in or by it. The fact that there is *always* an idea behind everything is *logical in nature.* Kant would use the term 'transcendental' to describe this condition because the use of sensibility, which relates us to individual entities, involves understanding. When, in trying to describe knowledge, we speak of human faculties, he says we resort to *transcendental analysis.* I am not sure that this analysis is appropriate here. The relationship between a particular and an idea is a logical one: there exists always a general conceptualization of what is considered in a particular case. The particular falls *a priori* under some idea. This subsumption can always be made and we always do make it, sometimes quite unconsciously. Such subsumption can always be made explicit. In fact, everything can always be conceived, wrongly or not, in terms of something more general of which it is a particular case. The particular refers back to the universal, that is, to a concept beyond which nothing else can be found since it is universal. As such, these universal entities function as principles. The striking fact is that the relation of involvement is quite *a priori*: something particular is always particular with respect to something universal; thereby, a principle is implicitly instantiated in the particular and can thus be 'seen' through (or in) the particular. Hence we often find an ideological causality at work in human activities: we cannot prevent ideas from arising and from being stimulated by our individual actions, let alone from what we say *hic et nunc.* Hence it is necessary to take ideas into account when we act, speak, or write. Ideological causality is precisely the act of conveying general ideas through *particular* actions. Such causality is always at work in human affairs, even when it is not specifically intended. Ideological manipulation, for instance, requires some degree of blindness on the part of the manipulated, a condition only possible due to an ideological causality which makes everything we do and say an instantiation of ideas, intentional or not. The rhetorical impact of literature is ideological in this sense: it aims at suggesting ideas through particular cases. A story, novella, poem, or other literary work represents a particular case that *illustrates* an idea which is implied as a rhetorical effect of the textuality of the literary work. When this implication is made explicit, we have an interpretation of the text. The idea(s) developed is (are) of a universal nature, they are *values*. After all, the moral of the story is, explicitly or not, of such an ideological nature.

As discussed earlier, our minds are ideological in the sense that we always relate what we see, touch, or feel to an underlying idea or principle that generalizes our information. We imperceptibly and indirectly obtain such ideas. Children, for example, learn and behave ideologically. That is why the old saying 'Do what I say, but not what I do' is self-defeating in pedagogical matters. The maxim is an inconsistent idea, and as a result, it cannot pretend to represent a guiding principle of children's actions. Parents will meet with serious difficulties in gaining respect from their children if they despise or simply neglect their own parents. The idea 'One should respect one's parents' does not force itself upon the child's mind, as an *idea*, when he or she can *see* it contradicted in one's own parents' actions and attitudes. Whatever the parents may say, the child is bound *to see* that the saying is not an idea or a principle, but a partisan and *ad hoc* discourse. Three basic features, therefore, characterize ideas:

(a)   ideas are universal and can serve as principles which are beyond questioning;
(b)   they can be conceptualized through judgments;
(c)   they are embodied within particulars, a condition that is necessarily so for Aristotle and contingently so for Plato.

Only such an embodiment permits us to see *what* is particular, thereby perceiving this *whatness*, which is itself universal and essential. The particular, therefore, reveals itself *as* particular thanks to the universality that it illustrates by phenomenalizing it.

4.2. *Ideas and questions in Plato's theory*

Plato was led to develop his theory in reaction against Socrates (cf. Meyer 1980). At first, it may seem odd to view Plato's ideas in this manner when we know how greatly Plato was influenced by Socrates' teaching and by his strength of mind and his courage, especially when facing death. In reality, the nature of the relationship between the two men was more complex. After all, good disciples seldom become great masters. We can doubt that Plato was unconditionally Socratic or that his Socrates was the one who actually existed.

For Plato, Socrates' ideas had as an unsatisfactory consequence the impossibility of answers. Everything was questionable; no conclusion could be drawn from a debate, which was therefore bound to remain aporetic. However, we see Socrates answer and reject answers. This can only happen if we presuppose some knowledge of what counts as an answer and what has to be rejected as not being an answer, such as a contradiction, for instance. How, then, could *everything* be a question in the last analysis? Even if Socrates allowed for a difference between questions and answers, the very fact that any answer could be turned into a question so that no dialogue could ever be brought to an end, and thus had to remain aporetic, led to the unwanted conclusion that there was no sharp dividing line to be drawn between questions as such and answers as such. An answer was, contrary to its proponent's *opinion*, a concealed question to be revealed as such by Socrates' *elenchos*. The main objection that can be leveled against such a view, if Socrates' attitude was developed into a view at all, is that one cannot determine when one has reached an answer. After all, the goal of a questioning process is to find an answer to the question initially raised. In Socrates' view, however, no room is left for answers or for a clear demarcation line between answers and questions, no proposed answer could ever be rightfully claimed to be more than the answerer's pretentions or delusions.

In fact, Socrates would not have minded these objections. His aim was not to lay down any theory of questioning, let alone reflexively to conceptualize the *logos* as he practiced it. His sole goal seems to have been to unmask the elders' social pretentions for what they were, that is, to undermine their avowed claim to power in the city based on their alleged knowledge of what virtue is. The virtue the elders possessed, or that they said they had, served to legitimate their power in the eyes of those they ruled. When asking the elders what virtue was, Socrates was not really interested in the true answer to the question. By simply showing that the elders themselves could not answer it without contradicting themselves, he wanted to show that they too did not know what virtue was. Consequently, how could the elders claim that they were entitled to the highest position in the Athenian city, when they justified this position by the possession of something they could not even define? At least Socrates, who also did not know what virtue was, did not make such a claim to power. The elderly citizens should have acted in a similar and consistent way.

Plato must have, undoubtedly, been in sympathy with Socrates' criticism of the Athenian structure of power. He must have admired Socrates' courage in the face of death, which was the consequence of Socrates' repeated attacks on the notables. But Plato could not accept Socrates' undermining questions for long. Not only because he himself became dogmatic, as we know *a posteriori*, but also because he rejected the conception of questioning as an equalizing procedure in which partners are alternatively questioners and answerers, *independently of their social roles*.

Someone who opens himself to questioning must necessarily account for what he says, and people in power, more than others, do not like to have to justify themselves and admit that their answers could be doubted.

More fundamentally, Plato rejected questioning as practiced by Socrates because Socrates was unable to *say* consistently what he was doing and indeed *could* not have provided a consistent account. How could one defend a question view in which one gives effective answers while, at the same time, one denies the existence of these answers? What value could a theory of questioning have if it did not allow one to tell the difference between questions and answers, but rather asserted that answers are disguised questions, i.e. not answers at all? Finally, how could we base any theory of knowledge, even of the knowledge of virtue, on questioning, since (a) questioning is essentially paradoxical,[19] (b) the lack of any problematological difference prevents one form ever knowing when one has reached an answer, and (c) what serves as an answer in a particular case depends upon the particular question asked, and the question itself is in turn no more than the measure of the questioner's state of ignorance. If knowledge had to be defined in terms of the questioner's ignorance, it would be as subjective as ignorance. True knowledge is knowledge independent of what one ignores or does not ignore. But questions are in fact raised in response to what we do not know. Questioning then appears as totally contingent and variable from individual to individual according to one's state of ignorance and knowledge.[20] How can questioning have a founding role in the constitutive process of knowledge?

Plato did not reject the usefulness of questioning; he simply relegated it to a minor and secondary role. *What* is in question emerges during questioning and remains as *what* is in the answer. This 'whatness' is called an *idea*. Questioning enables us to remind ourselves of some idea we already have in mind: it furnishes the opportunity for ideas to arise and come to the fore in our consciousness. Answers, on the other hand, bring ideas into play. Being present both in questions and in answers, ideas are independent of questions and answers; questions and answers simply render them explicit. Questions are mere triggers;

they are accidental and dependent upon variable subjects, whereas ideas are
eternal and essential.

If Plato, in some sense, killed Socrates, the questioner *par excellence*, both
must be seen as having had incorrect views of questioning. Socrates' view seems
to have been the main cause of the subsequent devaluation and rejection of
questioning.[21]

Despite the attitude of his master towards questioning, Plato developed a
theory of ideas which is of great use to problematology and which, contrary to
what he so strongly affirmed, does not replace questioning but is rather complementary to it.

If we carefully observe the structure of Platonic dialogues, there can be little
doubt that a theory of ideas had to result from them since ideas and dialectical
structures are intrinsically related. Let us consider again (9) and (10). There
are several ideas involved in (10), for instance. Among them, we could cite the
idea (i.e. *what* is in question) of a suggested accusation, of a request for the
interlocutor to do something, of a lack of responsibility on the part of the
speaker, and so forth. These ideas remain present whatever answer the interlocutor gives to (10). If we consider (9) and its answer

(9´)   Then let's go to lunch

we see right away not only that the idea is to go to lunch, but also that other
ideas are involved. The idea of bringing to an end the meeting of the interlocutors involved in the dialogue and the idea of eating something are lurking behind
the idea of it being one o'clock (cf. Plato's concept of division).

The fact that ideas are lurking beneath the surface of dialectical interaction
and are present in questions as much as in answers renders dogmatism possible.
In Plato's later dialogues, for instance, we see a questioner who uses his interlocutor's questions as pretexts and triggers for putting forth as answers statements that are independent of the questions asked and which represent the
a priori beliefs of the questioner. The question-answer relationship between the
protagonists does not really conceal the fact that certain ideas constitute the
actual message one of the interlocutors seeks to impart. This message is not
necessarily affirmed explicitly, but it is *what* is in question in what is said.
Ideas emerge out of dialogues as the universal behind the particular topics in
question in the dialogues.

The truth of the matter is that ideas and question-answer complexes are
closely related, as can be gathered from Plato's dialogues, but not to the extent

that they are substitutes for one another. In fact, such a substitution is impossible. The relationship between ideas and question-answer complexes can be explained only on the basis of the question view of language; even the illusion that question-answer couples are unessential with respect to the ideas to which they are related rests upon some features of questioning.

Ideas are *shown* (in the Wittgensteinian sense) within dialogues, such as these of Plato. They are the natural results of the autonomization process inherent in language. As Plato said, ideas emerge as the informative content of question-and-answer exchanges. Answers become apocritico-problematological entities by becoming detached from the questions which originally gave rise to them. To resort to a grammatical distinction, ideas relate *what-ness* to *that-ness*. The little word *that* introduces propositions in indirect speech. In dialogues, that-ness shows up *indirectly*, so to speak. Ideas are then conveyed, sometimes quite dogmatically, by being suggested by or derived from the dialectical exchange.

Since it refers to answers at a third-person level, a *that*-clause generates judgments, i.e. autonomized answers which can be used independently of their initial context and quite anew in response to other questions. Ideas are constitutive of statements, they manifest the universal in the particular by letting the particular appear as such, i.e. for *what* it *is*. After all, a judgment is nothing other than a relationship between a particular and a universal, as are names and predicates. Whatever can be said of judgments, they always express ideas. Many things could be said about the relationship between what is universal and what is intentionally devoted to particularization in the apophantic structures, but the very existence of the synthesis between the universal and the particular bears witness to the presence of ideas. The ontological status of ideas is of no concern to us. Ideas are what corresponds to *that-ness* in question-answer coules and are therefore a special type of answer that can also appear in dialogues (about ideas). Their mode of identification does not require from human beings that they be in contact with a 'third world' (Popper) of entities-in-themselves.

4.3. *Ideas and political ideologies*

Our mind is essentially ideological. Plato and Kant have insisted so much on this feature of our mind that it hardly needs further explanation. It is little wonder, then, that we also need and use ideas to guide our political attitudes as well as to justify and systematize our beliefs. This is ideology *stricto sensu*.

Let us now take a further step in our analysis of ideology in order to determine what makes ideology 'ideological', that is, politically oriented. Some examples will illustrate the point:

(a) Once upon a time, there was a scholar who had been accused of plagiarism by colleagues from another university. The facts were made public in some specialized journal of the scholar's field and were considered irrefutable by all those who took the trouble of reading the two texts in question, which were presented in the form of two juxtaposed columns in the journal. The plagiarist was not fired and even received tenure. One can only understand this paradoxical move in terms of the principle of ideological causality. The plagiarist's colleagues had appointed him primarily for his merits. When the facts became known to them, they promoted him, though it could have been legally possible and deontologically necessary to get rid of him. But, if they had canceled his appointment, his colleagues would thereby have recognized that they had been wrong and badly informed, that is, that they had not done their job correctly. But how *could* they have been wrong when their positions and titles indicated that they had the necessary and required competence to tell whether or not someone's work is good? By firing their colleague, they would have *shown* and suggested *that* they were not so competent. *This* idea would have perhaps never been explicitly mentioned as such, but the question of their titled ability to give authorized judgments would nevertheless have been questioned.

(b) A reverse case. Why were Galileo or Socrates condemned? After all, Galileo was not the first thinker to spread theories which did conform to those advocated by the Church. The Church survived and assimilated the successive developments of science. Why, then, did the Church react so extremely in the case of Galileo? As a hypothesis, the heliocentric theory could have been reconciled with the Holy Scriptures, and if Galileo had admitted this, he would probably have had less trouble (at least if we believe Bertolt Brecht). But to claim that Copernicus' theory was *true* suggested that those who defended opposite views were *wrong.* How could churchmen admit being wrong when they claimed to know God's message and to implement His teachings on earth? It was not so much the theoretical and abstract content of Galileo's cosmological doctrines that really embarrassed the Church at that time: who cared for those doctrines in everyday life? Rather, it was the fact that the priests *could* be wrong that upset the Church. If they were wrong about the nature of the universe, why could it not be that the prescriptions they imposed on the running of everyday matters involved a falsification of life? The idea suggested by Galileo's views was not cosmological, but political. The Church could be wrong; the question of its being right in matters other than cosmological doctrines was thereby raised.

The same interpretation holds for Socrates. Was he put to death because he had some particular ideas about virtue he shared with the youth? Or was he rather condemned for having shown quite indirectly that those who claimed to be virtuous were unable to define what virtue was, other than the ideological ground for legitimating their rule over the rest of the City? By revealing contradictions inherent in the elders' assertions, i.e. their inability to justify what they pretended to be and to have, Socrates undermined the power of the notables of his City, thereby suggesting they should not have been entrusted with political positions for which they could not provide a consistent account. In fact, those elderly citizens felt threatened by Socrates when he asked them to account for what they felt was self-evident and should have remained unquestioned. Their legitimacy in holding power and in being what they were was itself beyond all possible justification. The elders did not care much for virtue and justice, which receive a defined *social* content in all societies, no matter how implicit and ungeneralizable such ideas may be because they presuppose specific instances. Those elders did not feel it was necessary to give precise and explicit definitions of those imprecise, and always particularized, social notions – but then who does? So much the better if someone emerges to do so, *provided that the idea conveyed by such a conceptualization does not indirectly suggest the elders' ignorance.* In fact, as we all know, Socrates did not aim at reaching definitions of virtue and justice – much to the despair of Plato, who saw no point in raising questions if it were not to get answers – but at unveiling the rulers' lack of legitimate claims to authority, at revealing the questionable nature of their rule. But, of course, those notables could not say all this without raising the very question they wanted to avoid drawing attention to. They did not want to condemn Socrates for the literal content of his discourse but only for the ideas it suggested; on the other hand, they could not condemn him for what his ideas suggested, so they did condemn him on the basis of the literal content of his views.

What do these examples reveal about the nature of ideas making up political ideologies? Essentially this: those ideas should never be called in question lest this lead to the development of an open confrontation.

Such a confrontation would lay bare the ideological nature of the ideas under attack, without saving their ideological content, since the ideas in question already constitute the ultimate authority. The debate cannot be settled, and what is legitimated by the ideas now under attack necessarily becomes as problematic as these ideas themselves. The purpose of ideology is precisely to conceal the groundlessness of the grounding ideas that ensure the credibility of the rest of the society's ideas and beliefs. Ideology, understood *stricto sensu*, i.e. as political, is a legitimation system. It is nothing but a particular way of handling ideas, any idea actually, so that some reality, also captured by ideas, remains unchallenged, that is, out-of-the question. Even when the goal is to attack an ideology, such an attack requires in turn some ideological ground which must remain stable and hence covertly *ideological.* As discussed earlier, to mention something is to raise a question about it, to bring it into existence as a question, even if this mentioning or affirmation amounts to the question's solution. However, this alone is sufficient to show that the question deserved to be and actually could be raised.

One method our minds use to give ideas an ideological bearing is to auto-nomize one or several ideas with respect to the grounding ideas of the legitima-tion system. How could the problem of the relationship between *oberbau* and *unterbau* have ever arisen if ideology did not use this method of autonomy (or concealment)? The problem of the relationship between 'superstructure' and 'infrastructure', however, cannot receive a general solution, despite the usual mechanistic assumptions of the matter. Each particular situation manifests a specific occultation giving rise to a definite set of ideas more or less autonom-ized with respect to what makes that situation particular. Does this fact imply that there are no general features that can be identified? Actually, ideology obeys a logic and obeys certain rules inherent in its own nature and function. We shall pay attention to this logic in the next section.

Now, why must the ideas composing the backbone of ideology *stricto sensu* never be in question at all? After all, an ideology also defines itself by its closure, i.e. its ability to offer an answer to *any* question which could arise or be of any concern. In fact, political ideas function as groundless grounds: out of all avail-able ideas, some are definitely for such an ideological purpose. Like all ideas, they are principles, but, in a certain sense, are more so. They have a legitimizing role though they are themselves deprived of the legitimacy that they bestow on everything else that they legitimize. In functioning as the source of legiti-mation, these ideas cannot be legitimate, i.e. they cannot apply to themselves the criteria of legitimacy they define, without falling into a *petitio principii*. Instead of being grounded by ideas more fundamental than themselves, these ideas are illegitimate in their own terms, i.e. reflexively. This, as we may easily imagine, is a rather awkward condition for the ideas of an ideology *stricto sensu* to be in.

As a consequence, whenever one speaks of such ideas, even if it is in a positive way, they appear to be in question; they are being rendered explicit in what is said according to the problematological theory of language. These ideas must therefore remain in the background of what is explicit in order to fulfill their mission without danger. Thus they can play their role of unquestionable assumptions. These ideas are unlegitimated, and it is more appropriate for them to remain in the background. They must remain implicit *as such*, while manifesting themselves in a derivative way, lest they emerge in their nakedness, i.e. as purely *ideological*. What Socrates and Galileo did, for instance, was to question the dominant ideology of their time by suggesting that it was merely ideological. Ideologies, taken as political realities, must remain hidden in their ideological nature. A political ideology, being groundless and deprived of the legitimacy it bestows upon everything else, is invalid according to its own standards; hence these standards necessarily do not apply to ideology itself. Ideas can be suggested and rhetorically implied, but politically, the risk is that they may appear for what they are, i.e. groundless. It is therefore essential that ideology, political ideology to be more precise, does not reveal its nature as being *ideological*. If this ideological nature were unmasked, suspicion could only arise as to the ultimate reasons supporting the ideology. The ideas of political ideologies cannot be directly stipulated; they cannot even appear *as such* in discourse. Rather, they must be put forth under some mask, i.e. as particularized. The question of the validity of such ideas must neither be tackled, nor even mentioned, and the ideas themselves must not even be indirectly debated. They simply must be *transformed*. Here, I emphasize the word *form* in *transformed*.

An idea pertaining to some ideology must remain covert to be operational and should avoid being questioned since it cannot prove that it is valid, i.e. that its theoretical validity is unquestionable. After all, Socrates, Galileo, and those who discovered the case of plagiarism mentioned above did not directly question any ideology. They suggested ideas. Why were these people deemed 'dangerous'? Simply because they were putting the ideas of some dominant ideology *into question*. They were not suggesting that the ideas composing these ideologies were wrong or false, but they were implying that these ideas *could* be dismissed since they were problematic. It was this very idea their opponents could not stand, and that they reacted against accordingly, i.e. ideologically.

To sum up, some ideas are used ideologically, which means that they act as legitimizing agents. The specific characteristics of these ideas that mark them off from other ideas are that they should never be mentioned or alluded to. This is what the advocates of the ideology fear most of all. To avoid the disruptive effect attendant on making ideological ideas explicit, these ideas are repressed through a displacement into other ideas which simultaneously conceal and validate them. The process of validation takes place by means of an illustration of a more general principle which is never stated nor alluded to. But the illustration is nonetheless presented as one of the principle's consequences. Instead of *presented* one should rather say *represented*: one represents the principle in question, but as out-of-the question. As discussed previously, our mind is ideological *lato sensu*. Ideology *stricto sensu*, i.e. as a set of ideas used for legitimation purposes, is merely a derived employment of particular ideas. These ideas then manifest identical features throughout their possible usages. Consequently, all ideas *can*, but do not have to have an ideological bearing *stricto sensu* ("Everything is political," one often reads), and this leads to an autonomizing process of ideas with respect to the basic ideas of the legitimation system and thus a concealment of the basic ideas, i.e. a concealment of their own political roles. Another consequence: ideas, as we find them in ideologies *stricto sensu*, also relate the universal to the particular, even though this process of *representation* takes place through the mediation of another idea. After all, the 'signifier' can denote a 'signified', which, in turn, denotes no 'thing' by repeatedly signifying another 'signifier', and so on. To write is to read and to read is to write. Nothing is ever referred to individually, but rather, everything is always particularized through universal means *representing* the universal with the help of the particular. Language is an immense substitutional process in which there are always opportunities, thanks to the questions raised in texts through naming and predication, to refer to the real world, i.e. to enquire about it. *Reference* to an unsignifying signified is simply a stop in the substitutional chain of language resulting from another type of questioning process in which the entities referred to do not function any more as giving rise to signs. These entities become problematic. What is said ceases to appear as apocritical and turns into something in need of an answer that language can only encapsulate *a posteriori* and by means of substitution. Language, then, only functions when the problem of reference and referents is not raised, or as soon as the problem ceases to be raised since its solution is not linguistic.

4.4. *The logic of ideology*

Ideology presents itself as a world view. Hence it is global and closed. Two fundamental requirements dictate the logic of ideology:

(a)   ideology's pretension to answer all possible questions; and

(b)   its requirement that it never be directly under the fire of questioning.

How can one possibly answer *all* possible questions and *a priori* remain out of the question? Furthermore, a thought system cannot answer, i.e. say, everything without admitting contradictory statements as answers. How will the ideological system give the illusion of being consistent and *a priori* valid? This challenge gives us the key to the logic of ideology. In due time, we will also have to remind ourselves of what has been said in the previous section, namely that ideological causality can be characterized as an implication. In the case of the plagiarist, what was implied was the idea of the incompetence of his deceived colleagues. Since the plagiarist's colleagues could not allow such a conclusion to be drawn, they acted as if their colleague was not a plagiarist. What they really feared was not so much the fact that they had appointed a plagiarist, but rather the general idea *that* such an appointment *meant*, that is, *implied*. This is how ideological causality works, and the examples of it could be multiplied indefinitely.

The principle that governs ideological causality has its roots in the paradoxical requirement of ideology recalled at the opening of this section. In fact, ideological causality is but one aspect that a logic of ideology has to account for. The paradoxical requirement, as I called it, stipulates the necessity for such a logic to explain the ideological closure and the concealment of the nature of ideological presuppositions as ideological. The *fourth* feature to be taken into account is the particularization of general, ideological, presuppositions.

Let us now assume, for the purpose of the exposition, that we have one such idea or unquestionable presupposition that must remain concealed and *always* verified because it pertains to some given ideology *stricto sensu*. Let us consider an example of such an idea.

In a hypothetical primitive tribe, the high priest explains the fact that it rains by saying that he has pronounced the adequate ritualistic incantations. This means that he has the *power* to cause the rain to fall because he *knows* how to please the gods. One could easily demonstrate that there is no causal relationship between the rites performed by that priest and the falling of the rain. In order to provide such a demonstration, it would be necessary and sufficient to show that it has rained independently of the high priest's prayers and that these prayers did not cause any rain.

We may think that our demonstration will convince the priest in question that there is no relationship between his rituals and the weather. However, he will not accept our demonstration because it would challenge his role in society. Will the priest's tribe accept the demonstration? Again, from a social point of view, we can affirm that it will not: the tribe needs water for survival and does not know how to make it rain, so the tribe relies on somebody they trust to influence *Deum sive Naturam*. However, cultural barriers (gaps?), such as the fact that the concept of demonstrating something may be alien to the tribe, do not really account for the tribe's insistence on the efficacy of ritual power; rather, we know that people in our own, modern societies, including two-level scientists, believe in all sorts of things, including political and religious ideologies that do not allow one to consider alternative explanations or do not accept the fact that the ideology may be questioned. In spite of their claim to take all factors into account, these ideologies are in fact totally closed. How do they succeed and where does the illusion come from?

Let us suppose we present our demonstration to our high priest. He could easily discard what we regard as a proof that his ritual does not affect the weather. For instance, he might say that the gods have not listened to his prayers because they were angry at his tribe for some sin or other. This explanation even reinforces his priestly power, since he must now cleanse the people of their sins so that the rain will return. To explain why the gods sent the rain to the tribe, when he had not performed the usual rites, the priest could just as easily say that the rain was a reward for a previous action or silent prayer. After all, the gods are almighty and do not have to comply immediately with the priest's requests. Indeed, the gods listen to the priest but act when it pleases them to.

Thus, whatever happens, the priest is able to find a confirmation of his ideology and, therefore, of his role as a mediator between the humans and the gods in the weather and all other social events. The fact that it does rain after the priest's ritual implies that his religious creed[22] is valid, and the fact that it does not rain after the ritual can also be explained in terms of the creed. The creed can never be called into question because no alternative is left open which could falsify it. The creed is literally out-of-the question. However, we gather the impression that the question of the creed's validity is, indeed, raised and that we are faced with it in view of the particular question of whether or not it will rain. If p conditions the truth of q, even if p means q to the extent that the occurrence of the rain after the high priest has performed his rituals means that his creed is true, then one can reasonably expect that not-p should at least call q into question, that is, evoke not-q. This situation is however, ideologically excluded. We shall now see how the rhetoric of ideology works logically.

The question $q?$ that addresses the validity of the priest's acts and beliefs is actually never raised. It does not exist logically as a question. Such a question, being a yes/no question (also called propositional question) like all questions concerning the validity of existing propositions,[23] should admit q or not-q as answers. But q is always presupposed and not-q always excluded. Moreover, $q?$ seems to be *solved* by p (or not-p) as if $q?$ *meant p?*, and p also *implies q* as well as not-p. If not-p is the case, then p means q and implies q at the same time. Besides, p and not-p are presented as *consequences* of q, as its *manifestations*: the power of the gods is *represented* by the rainfall as much as by the absence of rain.

Let us now summarize our example in order to characterize the mechanism of rhetorical logic. p symbolizes the rainfall, and not-p the non-occurrence of the rain; q symbolizes the idea that the gods listen to the high priest and that they cause rainfall.

(a) *If q* is turned into a question, then p and not-p are the answers to $q?$.

(b) *If q?* is thought of as a question, then it materializes itself as $p?$. Since the answers to $p?$ are p or *not-p*, these are also the answers to $q?$.

(c) *p?* expresses a real alternative whereas $q?$ does not because, for $q?$, only one of the two theoretically possible answers, q and *not-q*, is allowed for.

(d) Can q turn into a question? The truth of the matter is that p and not-p raise the question q for the tribe, whose members believe that the rain is due to the gods via the mediation of the high priest. p is possible, not-p is possible, and $p?$ means the question of q; thus it follows that q is questioned, although indirectly. On the other hand, since $q?$ is never raised other than rhetorically, once can also say that q is considered *a priori* as a solution and as being confirmed.

The impression or *illusion* of giving a solution to $q?$ is due to a *petitio principii*. If a question has two answers which are actually nothing but the re-statement of the original question, one can say, as Aristotle did, that the proposition expressing the question, namely q, is not actually solved. That 'solution' results from a fallacy which consists of taking for granted what is supposed to be proved, namely q, by assuming that it is an *established premise* of a reasoning process which *concludes* with the validation of the premise. The conclusion could not have been reached without its having been taken for granted right from the beginning, and thus it is fallacious. In other words, the existence of the priest's gods is proved by the presence and the absence of the rain while, at the same time, the presence and the absence of rain are supposed to prove divine causality and the subsequent necessity to induce the goodwill of the gods via a well-introduced mediator.

The logic of ideology consists of assuming as solved a problem which, by being presupposed as solved, is then a pseudo-problem. The answers to the problem are real answers in the sense that they embody a real alternative, i.e. refer to *another* question. However, these answers are in fact not answers to the *initial* problem, but rather embody an alternative which expresses the initial idea, rather than constituting a solution to the idea's problematization. The logic of ideology succeeds in passing them off as answers to a question when actually no problem has been raised as such.

The logic of ideology is based on the illusion that a question has actually been asked when the ideas involved do nothing but close the system upon itself, allowing *all* questions (relevant to the ideology) to be asked when only a *limited* number of unquestionable presuppositions are involved that are *rhetorically* answered and are used to answer these questions. Quite obviously, this process enables the logic of ideology to meet the challenge of answering all questions while never itself being questioned as an ideology. The other requirements previously discussed are also met: the general idea, e.g. the religious ideology of the primitive tribe, is particularized into some *representative consequence*, namely, in our example, the presence or absence of the rain. This particularization enables our local *shaman* to offer an indirect justification for his ideology by displacing the problem of the validity of his creed by another idea. This new question is directly related to an observable phenomenon and hides that ideology under a non-rhetorical question.

At a deeper level, we can see that the logic of ideology stems from problematology. The fundamental feature of questioning which renders it possible is the problematological difference. Ideology pretends that two problems, i.e. two equivalent problematological answers,[24] are not equivalent. One of the two propositions derives from the other. The problematological difference must then, however fallaciously, prevail between the two expressions since they are substitutable. Implication is the means through which the problematological difference is created. The concealment of the equivalence between the two expressions generates an ideological effect. The idea presupposed is presented each time, whatever the circumstances, i.e. the consequences. The double implication that characterizes the substitutability of statements is reduced to a single implication. Instead of seeing some identity, we have an impression of otherness caused by the problematological difference. The role of this 'one way implication' is that of a problematological differentiator which creates the fiction that a real problem exists. Ideology creates fiction. Far from having anything to do with the opposition between referential and non-referential discourse, fiction is characterized by being an ideologically marked question-answer complex.

5. THE NATURE OF LITERARINESS

5.1. *Ideas and textuality*

Ideas are neither questions nor answers. Plato showed that they were presupposed by both. If ideas are given theoretical prominence, questioning can be discarded as inessential since neither questions nor answers differ as far as ideas are concerned. However, this view is misleading. Ideas can only emerge problematologically and apocritically from dialogues because of the autonomization of *what* is said in what *is said*. The dialogical form of Plato's dialogues, which contain some of the most dogmatic views we can find in the history of philosophy, bears witness to the existence of an implied third person who derives the ideas which are embodied within the questions and the answers of Plato's protagonists from reading. Hence the logical necessity of the Platonic world of ideas, the Third World, as Popper called it, though for reasons different from mine. My contention is that an adequate theory of ideas ought not to be seen as a substitute for problematology. On the contrary, we should realize that ideas are not conceivable outside the theory of questioning. This theory explains why and how propositions can acquire autonomy, however relative this autonomy may be: *that-ness*, i.e. propositional entities, results from questioning. Who believes that propositions float in the Heavens of Truth?

Ideas owe more to questioning than their origin. Being 'in' answers as well as 'in' questions, as Plato said (*Phaedo* 75 d), ideas can relate to both. *What* is in question must also be *what* the answer is about if both the questioner and the answerer are to speak about the same thing.

Textuality is fundamentally ideological, and this feature is also rooted in its problematological aspect. Texts illustrate ideas, sometimes by using other ideas; at any rate, texts embody ideas. This embodiment is what we have called *representation*: textuality is representative of ideas. We can write the following formula:

$$\frac{\text{texts}}{\text{ideas}} = \text{representation}$$

Representation means the illustration of something general that is shown but not said. Texts show *that* . . . but do not say that they show it. They illustrate

something which can be *seen* through a particularized case, such as a poem
which might seem too personal to concern anyone but the poet. Conversely, one
sees a universal idea in its particular manifestation in the text. The idea is as
representative of particulars as particulars are of the general idea: we can always
represent one by means of the other. Concrete characters in Sartre's plays are
often the textual devices employed by the author to suggest something general;
thus, ideas are then *represented* on the stage and left for the reader to infer.
Individuals, too, are representative. The particular is understood as being particular in contrast to the universal. One consequence of this fact is that a Picasso
painting is as 'realistic' as any other painting and that Mallarmé's poetry enables
us to grasp something real as much as any other type of poetry does. A text
offers *something* which is *perceived* as particular and *thought* in its particularity.
Such a *thought,* necessary to the perception of the particular, nonetheless leads
us beyond particularity, to a point where the perception can be understood as
being *particular.* It is that unspecified idea or thought which is rhetorically
conveyed by the textuality of the text. The literary mode of discourse is only
one among many ways of presenting ideas. The question raised by texts (we will
now assume that there is only one in order to facilitate exposition) as texts is
precisely concerned with ideas. The text *asks* the reader to grasp it as a text.
However, the question of how the text is to be understood as a whole is not
literally asked *in* the text; rather, the text as such *is* this question, and we can
say that it is asked *by* the text *qua* text. Textual interpretation then relates the
particularity of a definite narration (a poetry, a novel, a story, etc.) to a more
general view the text embodies and of which the text is a logically particular
case. This particularization of the idea also entails that this idea is embodied in
the text, in the sense that *what* the text says implies something else which is
more general (ideological causality). Even when the author denies the general
view implicit in his text, an idea lurks in the background of the textuality that
makes it ideological. This is logically bound to be so. If some validity must be
granted to the view that the interpreters can understand an author's work better
than the author can himself, or to the structuralist view that the author cannot
understand what his text means, these views must be restated in terms of what
has been said about ideas. We may deny the existence of structural homologies
across geographical areas and the scale of time which would give *the* adequate
reading of folktales (Propp 1965), for instance, or myths (Levi-Strauss). We may
also discard the false conception that the author's unconscious intentions express the true meaning of his text. The reading of the *Critique of pure reason*
does not amount to a psychoanalysis of Kant. This may seem less obvious in

the case of literary texts, but there is no reason to think that *textuality* differs in nature depending on the nature of *texts*. Rather, what can validate the idea of *unintended readings* lies in the theory of ideas: some implications are not drawn, seen, or intended by the author, but rather, are only relevant in contexts the author could not anticipate.

Our point is that some texts pretend to be devoid of ideas and claim to be mere 'stories' to be read for entertainment only. Detective or love stories are well-known examples of such literature. However, the idea that no interpretation is needed to understand a text is already an idea. Being the answer to what is called for by the text, the idea is itself out-of-the question. On the other hand, it is treated indirectly *by* the text through some instantiation of the idea that enables the author to conceal the idea to the extent that the reader can dispense with the task of looking for it. But how does he know that there is nothing to look for? Where does this idea come from, if not from the text and its nature or content? This idea is not ideologically neutral: it suggests an idea of what literature is, or should be, namely entertainment. So much for *Ulysses* or *The magic mountain*. The idea of a literature-without-ideas is ideologically very useful to all those who want to conceal ideas or take some idea for granted; such a literature never actually exists. It is always ideologically expedient to convey a rhetorical effect devoid of any political or ideological relevance. It permits one to avoid endangering some political ideology. There is no such thing as *ideological neutrality*. One always suggests an idea, or at least enters into tacit complicity with an idea by not questioning it in an illustration, e.g. a story.

5.2. *Literature and political ideology*

All this naturally leads us to speak of ideology *stricto sensu* as constituting certain modes of discourse as literary. Literariness is an ideological reaction to the world or to an ideology that a text supports or attacks.

Our whole question now is to see how the process works itself out and to see why literariness is the most appropriate mode of ideological discourse under certain circumstances.

In his classical book, Iser (1978: ch. 3) presented the most generally accepted answer to our question.[25] Literature should be seen as a reaction to ideological deficiencies. All thought systems leave something unthought; literature fills the gap. The literary repertoire is based on the social and literary norms prevailing at the time of composition. They provide the ground (i.e. a *Wirklichkeitsmodell*) between the reader and the author. Literature itself is the discursive answer to problems that arise in ideologies. Literature, then, fills ideological gaps, stabilizes prevalent world views, actualizes possibilities that are neglected by these views, and finally, takes up excluded or negated standpoints. Besides using a vocabulary of norms and ideas common to the reader and the writer, literature draws on its own tradition, previous literary works and themes, which are modified in response to the ideological deficit literature seeks to balance out.

> "All thought systems are bound to exclude certain possibilities, thus automatically giving rise to deficiencies, and it is to these deficiencies that literature applies itself. Thus, in the eighteenth century novel and drama, there was an intense pre-occupation with questions of morality. Eighteenth century literature balanced out the deficiencies of the dominant thought systems of the time. Since the whole sphere of human relations was absent from the system, literature now brought it into focus. The fact that literature supplies those possibilities which have been excluded by the prevalent system, may be the reason why many people regard 'fiction' as the opposite of 'reality'; it is in fact not the opposite but the complement." (Iser 1975b: 24)

The example Iser gives can help us see the problems with his claim. In the eighteenth century, empiricism was the dominant ideology. The association of ideas leaves the subject in the background of the empiricist view, though the subject is a necessary entity since it unifies impressions and ideas. But such a unifying pole is itself outside the realm of experience. It is an entity that cannot be defined in the terms that define experience. The subject is the blind spot of empiricism. It is not itself an identifiable object of experience. Hence it becomes necessary for empiricism to conceal the subject in its non-empirical role. As a result, intersubjective relationships, morality, and social relationships can only raise questions for empiricism, questions which are bound to remain outside the dominant ideology and which only literature could and had to treat.

Iser's views on this are undeniably attractive. They are plausible. However, they do not survive under close scrutiny. First of all, Iser's notion of deficiency (*Defizit*) is far from clear: it covers a wide variety of heterogeneous factors. A thought system can neglect a possibility, for the reason that it cannot deal with *every* question. The *possibility* in question, in the thought system, could perfectly well be dealt with if that question *actually* arose. This is a first type of Iserian deficiency. A second type is illustrated by the example of the eighteenth century empiricist ideology. This second type involves an internal deficiency of the thought system, something that is *structurally* excluded by the ideology. We should realize that nothing proves that what is structurally excluded by a set of ideas ever had to be part of the ideology. Many ideas are simply discarded by ideological systems as being incompatible with the system. Does the logical exclusion of an idea by an ideology represent a deficiency of that ideology which must therefore be dealt with literarily? In addition, literature is often produced as a reaction *against* an ideology, as a covert means of combating the ideology and changing the minds of those who adhere or could adhere to it. We may have a perfectly coherent thought system and a literary reaction against it if, for instance, the political infrastructure on which the thought system is based is oppressive and repressive for those who would decide to speak freely and openly. Literature may then become the adopted mode of criticism, not because of some internal deficiency of the ideology, but, on the contrary, because of external constraints. Literary attacks that expose a deficiency do not necessarily arise in response to that deficiency of the ideology.

A second objection to Iser's ideas concerns the vagueness of his views on ideology. We do not know what ideology is and how it works in his theories. However, we do know that literature is not simply ideological, though we do not know the features it shares with any thought system. The specificity of literariness evades Iser's notion of deficiency and, more specifically, of ideology. What are the *sui generis* features of literature *as* ideology? After all, literature is no more propaganda than anti-propaganda.

> "The function of literary allusions is to assist in producing an answer to the problems set by the deficiencies ... They also 'quote' earlier answers to the problems answers which no longer constitute a valid meaning for the present work, but which offer a form of orientation by means of which a new meaning may perhaps be found."
> (Iser 1978: 79)

The last sentences of this quote are undoubtedly true, but Iser's framework does not enable us to say why they are to be considered as true. Deficiencies are now seen as *questions*. Unfortunately, Iser relies too heavily on Collingwood's theory of questioning without extending Collingwood's ideas or without seeing that they need to be refined. Collingwood's ideas on questioning are no more than programmatic and sketchy. The truth of the matter is that Iser only refers to questioning incidentally; he says too little about it and assumes too much. Iser does not see questioning as a grounding structure for literary (and non literary) discourse or even for *reading*. Iser's theory of questioning, however employed, is a presupposition which, in his view, does not need to be clarified. It only needs to be used when necessary, though we are not told why or when it would be necessary. Maybe questioning is not necessary after all.

Let us now recapitulate the questions that Iser's conception of literature immediately suggest and that any alternative theory will have to face:

(a) Why is literature the mode of discourse *appropriate* to deal with ideological deficiencies?

(b) If literature is a reaction to ideology, how can it survive its ideological environment and still move readers at other periods of history?

(c) Let us assume the first question solved. Why should literature be used to oppose an ideology?

(d) Why should ideological reinforcement or stabilization be left to literature? In other words, why would an ideology defend itself through literature, rather than through its own internal mechanisms of defense or resolution?

(e) The purpose of an ideology is to be all-encompassing and, thereby, to provide an explanation for any problem, including new, particular cases. Ideology is closed upon itself to the extent of being unfalsifiable (Popper). How could ideological deficiencies arise? Where are those 'virtualities and negated possibilities' (*virtualisierten und negierten Möglichkeiten*) with which literature must deal? An ideology aims to be all-encompassing: it is a huge, swallowing machine that does not allow any argument, or counterargument, to be tenable.

A brief comment on the significance of these questions. In (a), the question asked is how literature can actually continue the ideological struggle, given that literature is neither propaganda nor anti-propaganda. After all, we do not really see how this mission could be fulfilled by literariness, which is a heterogeneous mode of speech in contrast to ideological discourse. In (b), the nature of the relationship between ideology and literature is considered. What is the ideological structure of literature? How does it intrinsically affect or define literariness? (c) and (d) actually raise the problem of ideological deficiencies as being something literature reacts against and that are therefore *necessary* and *sufficient* causes of literature. In (e), we even question the existence of such deficiencies in ideology.

Literature is ideological in the broad sense of the term. Novels, stories, or poetry illustrate and exemplify. Ideas are indirectly manifested since ideas are not the explicit content of literature although they may the object of literature. In other words, literature conceals ideas as much as it embodies them; it does not stipulate ideas as being ideas but, instead, illustrates them or, rather, *repre-*

sents them. Thus ideas can become efficient (*Wirkungseffekt*) without being openly challenged or having to be defended. Politically, it is very useful to resort to such a mode of speech. We can then understand why literature can be ideological *stricto sensu* and how such literature works. We can even easily see why literature is intrinsically ideological *stricto sensu*; it conceals the ideas it advocates or criticizes by giving a *good* or *bad* example of these ideologies.

Does this mean that ideas are never subject to open discussion? Quite clearly, no. Ideas, political or not, can be put forth, maybe not *as ideas*, i.e. as embodying particular interests or conceptions. But surely they can also be expressed without having to be cast in the literary mode. What occurs in this case is the reverse of what happens in literature: the ideas that are explicitly stated are the embodiment of particular viewpoints or interests but, since they could not be accepted if they were simply propounded in their particularized form, they are phrased in general terms. Who is not in favor of Liberty or Justice, for instance? It is only when these ideas are brought into play in actual circumstances that disagreement may arise. Hence it is often advantageous to conceal specific circumstances in general formulations, i.e. into some non-fictional discourse where they are advocated as universal, and where the particular viewpoints can be treated as presuppositions that can be dispensed with by being considered. In other words, some specific and particular conceptions are justified by claiming that they embody universal ideas. These ideas remain questionable, even when they are put forward explicitly and non-fictionally, though they are meant to appear as evident, as out-of-the question, as being devoid of debatable content.

An open ideological debate is then paradoxical. On the one hand, ideas, like Justice or Virtue, are useless if left unspecified; on the other hand, such ideas, to be useful, must be specifically determined. But once they are particularized, they necessarily become questionable, precisely because this particularization is likely to appear objectionable from another possible and equally particular point of view. Hence the ideas under discussion are concretized within arguments with the aim of justifying a particular interpretation concerning the content of these ideas.

Now, why would an ideology unveil its presuppositions and thereby incur the risk of challenge and defeat? Here, I do not intend to answer this question, but simply to underline why the proponents of political ideologies are reluctant to take openly ideological stands. Rather, they prefer to resort to a specific mode of language that enables them to leave the essentials out of the discussion, while continuing to defend their basic principles through exemplification in a type of discursivity that does not leave room for *theoretical objections*. Though the ideas of political ideologies are essentially problematic, they must not appear problematic. Since ideas are the measures of our judgment, what alternative is left if, in a case of radical disagreement and conflict, no principle remains to decide between or resolve opposite viewpoints? One way of avoiding such a situation is to prevent the possibility of open conflict that would lead to it by illustrating the idea one wants to defend, instead of justifying it against some opposing manifestation[26]. The aim of such an illustration is to reveal the positive sides of the idea if one wishes to advocate it and its negative aspects if one wishes to challenge it. Literature certainly exemplifies these linguistic procedures.

We should be aware that, in many cases, it is impossible to determine which of the alternatives offered by opposite ideological statements is valid. To return to the examples mentioned above, one may be opposed to the existence of hierarchies or to the complacency of intellectuals, while being reluctant to give way to anti-intellectualism or the utopian hope of suppressing social hierarchies. Literature does not offer solutions, but points to some problematic situation raised by a socio-economical context that *renders* the prevailing ideologies somewhat deficient. This point enables me to turn to the questions I mentioned earlier in my critique of Iser's theory.

Basically, textuality asks for something. It raises a question for the reader to solve. Rather than being explicit, this question — or these questions — are rhetorically posed *by* the text, implied *by* it *in* what it declares. This is where ideas come in, since the text *represents* ideas, gives the ideas a particular context, and illustrates them along with the questions at stake in relation to the ideas. When the ideas pertain to some *political* ideology, literature accomplishes what is most essential for such a system of ideas: it does not identify the ideas as ideas. Rather, literature leaves ideas unquestioned in the background, while at the same time using a particular and illustrative case to put their alleged validity in question.

So much for ideologies which are defended. Literature does the job much better than open argumentation by staging an ideology's ideas quite indirectly, sometimes surreptitiously; explicit debate would force ideas to the barricades. Literary strategy is more subtle.

However, a text can exert a *control function* by raising questions, a phenomenon that is quite well-known to the theoreticians of questioning (cf. Goody 1978: 30); texts call some idea into question and represent it *as questionable*, though the ideology under attack considers the idea as already resolved and thus out-of-the question. Why, now, is recourse made to literature? The answer is quite obvious: to avoid possible repression or censorship. Literature can be used against an ideology in spite of any possible physical repression of the author or his work since literature is illustrative; it uses particularized narratives to underline problems far better than any theoretical and necessarily abstract debate can.

It is important to note here that, while ideologies are closed systems of thought that can face all problems by providing solutions that conform to the ideology's premises, these solutions may be artificial. The faithful will always be convinced, as history shows. No *rational* way remains open to challenge the ideology, and irony is the sole answer left. To use Frye's words, literature is intrinsically ironic to the extent that it *questions* the foundations of political ideologies by discrediting them in their own terms. This procedure can succeed where a non-literary method of attack is bound to fail because the non-literary method operates in a field where these ideologies have all the argumentative weapons at their disposal to crush the adversary.

To sum things up, literature raises questions through textuality. These questions relate to political ideology since they are raised as such, or since they provide answers that suppress the 'questionhood' of the ideas invoked, i.e. that represent the ideas as evident and legitimate through some exemplification which necessarily presupposes these ideas. The common feature between these two possible ways of relating to ideology through questions resides in the facts that (a) texts raise questions through textuality, (b) these questions call for answers that embody certain ideas, and that (c) political ideologies and social values are composed of ideas which, unlike other ideas, need to appear to be out-of-the question. As a result, texts have an ideological bearing, either by raising questions that ideologies are reluctant to acknowledge as questionable or by raising questions whose answers reinforce ideologies by exemplifying them. The truth of the matter is that questions are at stake in all thought systems, and that textuality consists precisely in asking for something. Literature enables mankind to match the demands of ideologies with the possibilities of textuality. This leads us back to Iser's views, which, as discussed earlier, pose more problems than they solve. All systems of ideas, political (i.e. functioning as the ground for the legitimation of social and political values, and their corresponding realities) or not, have gaps, which are not necessarily problems in their own terms. Even if they acknowledge such deficiencies, ideologies can nonetheless offer solutions that are quite consistent with their premises. An ideology can always do this. After all, it cannot cover *all* the possibilities of the questions which may one day present themselves.

The question view shows that ideologies rest upon problematic presuppositions and that, for ideologies to function, these presuppositions must appear unproblematic. Open justification of the presuppositions is always possible, but the weakness of this procedure is evident in times of crisis or incipient rebellion. Nothing lies beyond these ideology's presuppositions that could justify them and still pertain to the ideology. Literature, then, provides a good means of illustrating that which, though unfalsifiable, can never find an ultimate justification. Literature enables political ideology to name as answers the solutions it provides without having to say "Here are the answers", that is, without running the risk of putting the ideology into question by literally explicitating the ideology's grounding statements. Thus, literature deals not only with deficiencies but also with all the kinds of themes and subjects that one can find treated in thought systems. Furthermore, it does not deal with the possibilities left aside or excluded by ideologies but with the actual preoccupations of those systems. Both literary and non-literary texts can provide answers to ideological problems. The more indirectly the solution relates to the ideology's ideas, the greater the convincing power of such solutions, hence literary illustration's efficacy in dealing with ideological problems. When there is some deficiency, or rather, some problem in an ideology, literature may be the most appropriate mode of discourse to handle it, since literature is a system of answers that calls for other answers, a system of propositions that exemplifies answers problematologically. Literature answers by staging problems, that is, by asking something other than what is literally said. By not explicitly stipulating what is in question in its textuality, literature has an ideological impact since ideologies can be defined as systems of ideas which do not want to appear as such. Hence an ideology prefers to defend itself literarily and to operate at a level of literary representation at which general ideas can receive concrete expression.

The phrase *What is in question in literature is not literally stipulated* should be understood to mean that the question is not explicitly stated, but is rather inherent in the text that embodies it. It is an essential feature of textuality to raise such questions; the answers to the question are then asked *by* the text through the answers given *within* it. The question is then totally unspoken and *what* is problematic is not specified, i.e. is not stipulated by the text, which is simply made up of answers; hence the role of the reader. What is in question is not literally expressed, i.e. does not appear as in question, not even *in* what is said; the proposition dealing with what is in question is not literally present in the text, though the text does suggest it. From an ideological point of view, this enables the communication of ideas in a figurative fashion; they never have to be brought into focus as ideas, i.e. as intrinsically *questionable*.

Opposition to ideologies is achieved through the same means, that is, through the implication that something is problematic. However, contrary to cases in which ideologies are reinforced, the questions raised here allow ideas which must remain unquestioned to appear problematic. In so-called 'popular' literature, the idea is 'Don't ask questions because they're all there', the idea being not to question what is evident. Ideologies often become more subtle when they pass into literature. Literary texts can mean something corresponding to an answer in the ideology in question, or at least, can provide an answer related to that ideology. In the situation in which an ideology is challenged, the question raised by the text focuses on the questionable character of some ideas or the answers in the ideology. Hence irony can derive from such a procedure: the writer takes the ideology's ideas for granted, proceeds as if he accepted those ideas, and elaborates their undesirable consequences; or he can also propose an alternative solution. In the latter case, a question arises as to the necessary validity of the solution the ideology provides. Since it is closed upon itself, an ideological system does not admit the existence of questions or alternative possibilities; these fall outside the ideology's scope of justification and point to its inadequacy. The mere act of showing *that* an ideological solution is not necessarily a real answer *suffices* to challenge the very nature of the ideology. Since they exclude alternatives, ideologies resent questioning. Besides enabling authors to escape open censorship (or worse), literature also has the advantage of not having to offer a positive or general answer to ideological arguments, while it criticizes such arguments as ideological and ungrounded and questions their 'social validity'.

However universal literary discourse may appear, literature raises problems through particular cases and insofar as it addresses itself to sensibility (i.e. to what is specifically individual in each of us), even as, from the intellectual point of view, it appeals to our unconscious. My point here is that ideas are related to the unconscious, and that sensibility is related to consciousness. This idea is quite the opposite of one what one normally reads about literature. In agreeing with the conventional view, one fails to understand the functioning of ideologies.

Now, a final word about each of the questions posed earlier about ideology and literature:

(a) When ideological questions arise, literature is an appropriate means of dealing with them since textuality raises questions in an indirect manner, which is essential when one is dealing with ideology. Ideological problems must not appear as deficiencies in the ideology: they must rather be seen as problems.

(b) The ability of a literary work to become independent with respect to the ideological matrix from which it arises can be explained by the fact that, in dealing with problems, a literary work offers alternatives to the ideological closure and thus renders itself autonomous (or rather, appears autonomous) with regard to the thought system. The capacity of answers to acquire independence with respect to the question(s) which gave rise to them enables such autonomization of literary works. Literary works can therefore survive their epoch of origin.

(c) For several reasons, literature is the best means of making ideological challenges. Literature can conceal the threatening nature of such a challenge, and thus enable the questioning to escape censorship. Literature further enables critics to avoid having to offer an ideological alternative that they often do not have or are unable to put forth. Literature also permits the critics of a given thought system to focus on some particularly vulnerable aspects of the ideology in their attacks.

(d) When a problem arises for an ideology, it may be in the interest of the ideology concerned not to explicitly present itself as an ideology. It may be better to embody ideas in a literary discourse, a form of language more appealing to sensibility and one that can make the ideas appear legitimate.

(e) An ideology is always capable of resisting *rational* argumentation. The closure of a thought system can nonetheless be ruptured, and literature creates such breaks more convincingly than other forms of language. Irony for instance is hard to parry and withstands literal-minded critiques.

If we have begun to understand the nature of ideology and, more precisely, its logic, we can see why ideological systems, though being totally closed upon themselves, protect themselves by displacing their grounding theses by resorting to a mode of speech apparently autonomous with respect to the problems ideology deals with. Textual autonomy is a feature of both scientific and literary discourse. The basic difference between the two, as far as problematology is concerned, lies in the way they tackle problems. Science envisages problems as they are and hence needs a *method* of resolution. Literature answers problems by displacing and repressing their disruptive problematicity as if there had not been any problems at all to be solved. Fundamentally, the logic of ideology is merely an instantiation of rhetorical argumentation. In the third chapter, we have characterized rhetoricity as an indirect solution to a question. The nature of ideological logic as rhetorical argumentation could be illustrated by an example. Let us suppose we ask *Has John stopped beating his wife?* in order to imply that John is married. If this question were ideological, and not simply rhetorical, we would be able, *quod non*, to argue in favor of the opinion that John is a wife-beater without mentioning or making explicit that the question was even raised, let alone solved, by what we said. Obviously, our example is too much explicitly stated to be ideologically rhetorical. However, what the logic of ideology exemplifies is the general structure of rhetoricity: textuality is defined by the presence of questions that are non-literally posed in the answers provided in the text, although these questions are implied in some way, i.e. figuratively, by the text itself. A question is then indirectly at stake when we read a text and try to understand it beyond its surface structure by going beyond literal reading.

However essential its role in many other aspects may be, the logic of ideology is only a particular case of rhetorical textuality. The logic of ideology stipulates that the question that is debated be apparently, i.e. rhetorically, posed through some other question (a) that is supposed to express the real question, (b) that creates the illusion of expressing the initial belief, which must remain out-of-the question, in terms of an alternative, i.e. of a *real* question, and (c) that is actually a non-rhetorical question admitting the possibility of contrary solutions.

Insofar as rhetoricity is concerned, the specificity of the logic of ideology lies in its ability to create the fiction of a *result* or a *conclusion* with respect to a proposition that is held *ab initio* and that cannot ever be called into question effectively. Textuality is a rhetorical notion that implies that the questions that are indirectly asked are already answered as if those questions were not true questions. When the textuality of a text is ideological *stricto sensu*, such a particularization of textuality becomes effective.

We can see the logic at work in both cases of covert ideological responses, that is of literature as answers to ideological problems.

When an idea pertaining to some ideology is to be defended from possible questioning, two lines of defense are available. The idea can be directly justified; however, this requires that some more fundamental ideas be evoked. If these fundamental ideas are also under fire, the whole strategy breaks down because it leads to disagreement without appeal. Hence an ideology usually defends itself indirectly, by repressing the idea's universal nature and concentrating itself on a particular illustration of the idea that presents it as out-of-the question, as an answer beyond all possible doubt. On the other hand, an ideological attack proceeds in a reverse way: it does not offer direct opposition to the idea in question, but rather emphasizes some of the idea's questionable aspects. Instead of presenting the idea as 'the answer under all circumstances', it foregrounds it as a question by suggesting *that* the idea is actually called into question. The logic of ideology is at work in both ideological defense and attack. An answer is put forward that refers indirectly to a question that in the case of both ideological defense and attack cannot appear directly in the foreground. *Some other question* simultaneously expresses and represses the question. In the first case, the idea in question is presented *indirectly* as solved; if the actual solution were mentioned, this would imply that the idea in question *could* effectively be questioned. The *problematological displacement* of that question enables the writer to avoid this problem. In the case of an ideological challenge, the textual answer is propounded as inadequate with reference to some idea that the author thereby wants to call into question. The author does not directly question the idea being challenged but instead presents it as questionable through the textual answer he offers. To avoid validating the idea in question, the writer must not give answers that are answers to the idea in question. Successful ideological challenge can only be made indirectly, according to the logic of ideology. Ideological criticism, e.g. irony, functions then under a constraint: the answer about which the writer raises a question cannot directly answer that question, lest it thereby validate the idea by answering it. The negation of an idea cannot be directly presented, since it would be thereby become an open-ideological conflict and not a criticism. As a result, the answers must be the answers *to another question.*

5.3. *The dialectics of fiction*

The distinction between fiction and veridical discourse is usually made in terms of the so-called referential features of language, which, in principle, one can always characterize and recognize. In earlier chapters, we have seen that this distinction is untenable since language is referential, literary or not. Furthermore, we would surely hesitate to affirm that Zola's books, for instance, are less realistic than police reports or sociological descriptions.

Our rejection of any type of reference theory as grounds for the criterion differentiating literary and veridical discourse goes against the most deeply entrenched assumptions of literary analysis. However, we do not deny that fiction is a *sui generis* mode of discursivity. As such, it is intelligible in terms of the question view of language and more specifically as an implication of the rhetoric of ideology.

We find the rhetoric of ideology at work in literature because literature is an ideological necessity. Literature is not only one among several modes of discourse employed by ideologies to covertly promote their theses, but is also intrinsically related to ideologies as a necessary effect of their very natures. This might sound somewhat shocking to those who see literature only as a way of escaping everyday reality, as a source of aesthetic pleasure, and as an idealized expression of human affectivity.

Although literature undeniably does enable the reader to withdraw from the conventional world and to experience idealized forms of beauty and emotion, those who would define literariness according to its ability to do these things often fail to realize that these characteristics are only side effects of literature's basic grounding in ideology. While we avoid the reduction of literature to ideology, we should also refrain from envisaging literature as a purely autonomous discourse in which ideological features, if present, are purely incidental to its essence. In reality, the autonomy of literature is relative. Autonomy is itself a dynamic concept. Something is autonomous with regard to something else. The dynamic that links ideology with literature is a process of autonomization that can be described in terms of the rhetoric of ideology. Literature is characterized by an ideological response that affects literariness in the following way: literary discursivity becomes independent of ideology *stricto sensu* and thereby embodies new problems that it represents through particular examples. Such a *sui generis* representation of a *sui generis* sphere is called *poiesis*. We can also speak of the *poetics* of literary texts.

As we have seen previously, all the properties of literary discourse are useful for ideological expression. One might think that this is due to contingent factors. Who would deny that ideology benefits from literature? The truth of the matter is that literature *as such* would not have been possible without the existence of ideologies: for ideologies to survive and exist, it is necessary that they generate a *sui generis* type of discourse called fiction. Literary texts would not have come into existence if ideological problems had not arisen.

Mythologies are a good example of the necessity to relate an ideological question to a literary expression or answer. Myths are forms of literary discourse and sources of the literary themes of their time. They are also meant to justify a given social order by rendering it intelligible and necessary in terms of a narrated past. They embody examples and models for the present, understandable by their natural audiences. Mythological odes or stories are simultaneously literary and ideological. Why would this dual nature be found only in literary texts of the past?

The rhetorical logic of ideological discourse requires fiction. Ideology, in general, cannot be presented as ideology by its proponents. This would unveil ideology for what it actually is, namely particular viewpoints that are presented as being universal. In addition, this would incur the risk of calling into question what is intended to remain always out-of-the question. Ideological arguments are generally employed to conceal what is ideological in ideology. However, these arguments belong to a single level of discourse: they address themselves to an ideological question in a direct manner, that is, ideologically. They may provide illustrations or particular cases of an implicit idea, but they nonetheless solve the idea in question by justifying it in the face of claims that it is invalid. Literary texts, on the other hand, tackle the same ideological questions *indirectly*, by shifting to a different level of argumentation. Literature displaces a question by presenting another one that is apparently not ideological and answers the former by answering the latter. The effect of this problematological displacement is different from that of ideological argumentation: in the latter case, one answers an ideological question; the idea in question is actually submitted to a questioning process even if the idea itself is not directly mentioned. In the case of literature, the idea in question is never really questioned and therefore cannot be rejected, cast into doubt, or confirmed. The displaced idea is only rhetorically questioned, as in example (10); whatever the answer to the question displacing the ideological question is, it will confirm the original idea.

So far, we have taken literature for granted and have seen how it embodies an ideological rhetoric that is quite specific with regard to ideological texts. However, the fundamental question is: *why* did ideologies have to create fiction — that is, problems that are fictional with respect to the real problems of ideologies — and *how* was it accomplished?

In the example of our high priest, we encounter an open ideological argument. The existence of the divine was never really questioned, and when it was, this was done only rhetorically. Whether or not it rained, the weather always supports and instantiates the tribe's principles.

Now, let us suppose that the question of whether or not there is a link between rain and the existence of the tribe's god were raised: this third question must be resolved through a *mytheme*, which resolves all questions. So, other questions could arise without really creating any problem.

Inevitably, certain questions arise that must be answered by and within ideology. According to Iser, if this question poses a problem for the ideology concerned, two outcomes are possible: either the ideology can answer the question, or it cannot. If it cannot, the ideology *externalizes* its deficiency. The question is answered at another level of discourse where it no longer appears as irreducible from and as a deficiency of the ideology concerned.

There is something akin to a problematological displacement in this description, but Iser's account is unsatisfactory since it fails to take account of the rhetoric of ideology. Why would or should fiction result from the situation Iser describes?

According to the problematological view, there is no such thing as an ideological deficiency since ideologies are by definition capable of answering any external question, i.e. a question emerging from the particular circumstances of reality. Ideologies can always answer no matter however fallaciously. We see that the true significance of the closed nature of ideologies lies in the fact that it is due to the impossibility of providing valid answers to *all* questions; their failure to *really* take into account opposite claims, *real* alternatives, prompts *fictional* answers. Now, it is also true that ideologies cannot appear to be closed and therefore must appear to take questions seriously as questions. If an ideology simply offered an ideological solution held *a priori* as an answer to a question, it would reveal that the question had not been treated as a real one and that, whatever the question raised, the ideology could produce the answer.

Ideologies, therefore, require mediation. The function of mediation here is to rhetoricize *the idea* in *question* if the questions raised bear on some idea internal to the ideology, or – and this amounts to the same thing – to rhetoricize the non-rhetorical *question* with respect to the *ideas* of the ideology. The mediating discourse is necessarily fictional and autonomous: it is characterized by the rhetoricalization of a real question achieved through a process of displacement that makes the ideological relationship appear non-ideological.

Why must ideology answer indirectly if the question raised does not reveal a deficiency? Why is a mere ideological argument unsatisfactory? If an ideology does not directly answer a problem, does this not prove that the problem falls irreducibly outside of the ideology's realm of apprehension? Does it not mean that the ideology lacks the answer to the problem and that the problem must then be answered by another kind of solution, a solution at another level of argumentation and therefore expressed in another mode of language? Does the rhetoric of ideology not render mere ideological arguments impossible by always imposing the mediation of a fictionalizing problematic?

In reality, if a question directly challenges an ideology, or if it discloses a fundamental principle of the ideology, a problematological displacement is bound to occur. If, on the other hand, the question already has an answer whose stipulation does not unveil as ideological some ideological assumption, the ideology will not resort to fictionalization, i.e. to the rhetoricization of the problem raised. If there is no *real* question facing the ideology, there is no need to rhetoricize anything. But if the question is a real one coming from outside the thought system, it reflects a reality that must be incorporated and *thought* within the system; this can always be mastered, albeit indirectly, through a rhetoricizing of the question *or* of the idea to be presented as the solution to the question.

The rhetoric of ideology enables us to see when an ideological argument can be used and when it leads to a fictionalization of the question raised. If the question lends itself to a ready-made answer, or if it does not challenge an answer that is already present in the thought system and can be used to solve the question, then it will normally be answered directly though it does represent a real alternative or query. In other words, the real question is already rhetorical with respect to the ideology: the answer pre-exists the question, though the questioner ignores this fact. For him, the question is a real question but, with respect to the thought system, it is not really a question, but rather a stimulus for a ready-made discourse, one that does not challenge the validity of the ideas upon which it is based.

On the other hand, if the problem necessitates an answer that an ideology cannot offer without revealing its ideological nature, the ideology will transform the question into the form of another question that it can handle. Let us return to the example of the shaman. He obviously does not feel threatened by the question of whether or not it will rain since, in his ideology, whatever the answer offered, the gods remain the cause of what happens. The *mythology* of the tribe establishes the link between the gods and whatever occurs. The question of the rain is then rhetorical with respect to the priest's beliefs even if it is in itself a real question and even a question bearing on the real itself. Let us suppose that the shaman is faced with the question of whether or not his god exists. He could answer by citing the fact that it has rained *or* the fact that it has not. The circle of the ideological closure is perfect. The shaman can offer an ideological argument, 'without literature' so to speak, precisely because his argumentation draws upon a literature in the form of *mythemes*. The more an ideology incurs the risk of appearing ideological, by being distinct from literature as in our modern societies, the more it needs a literature as a complement.

Two cases, then, do not lend themselves to the open ideological treatment of a question. When the problem is to promote[27] a basic principle, the principle must be *assumed* true. The solution must not give the impression that the principle had ever been in question. The second case involves any question that would give rise to a solution that the ideology could offer, but which would reveal the ideology's capacity to always answer whatever question arises. Here, the rhetoricity of ideology must be transferred to another problem embodied within a different idea. This process is called *protective problematological displacement.* Literature, then, is not the product of deficiencies in thought systems but rather of their excessive power, i.e. of their unfalsifiable nature.

In sum, literature is the rhetoricization of an idea that raises a question in a specific manner. For an idea to be involved in this process, it must be too fundamental to allow for it to be defended as part of an ideology or for it be challenged directly. When a real question is raised that can still be handled rhetorically (i.e. without danger) by the thought system *in question*, there is no impediment to responding directly. Otherwise, a process will occur in which the question is fictionalized and indirectly rhetoricized with respect to the ideology.

All questions that can emerge as challenges to ideologies must naturally come from outside. For an ideology, reality in general is the permanent problem to solve. Ideology suppresses the real questions as real, *either* by answering them directly ideologically, *or* by suppressing their impact as challenges through a specific process of rhetoricalization. In the first case, the questions remain at the level of reality since the answer is homogeneous with the problem. In the second, the problematological displacement of the initial question trans*forms* this question (rhetoricizes it in terms of the ideology) and suppresses it into another one which, by definition, has not been *really* raised. An illusion of reality is created by means of that transfer, but the question that is used to replace the initial question is nevertheless a *fiction* with respect to this original problem. This is how *fiction* arises out of *reality.*

If, as we expect, the rhetoric of ideology is active in ideological arguments, it also provides the rules that, in the cases just mentioned, make it impossible for an ideological answer to be offered without the mediation and invention (*poiesis*) of a level of discourse which transforms and rhetoricizes the original question or the whole original problematic. An ideology must rhetoricize reality when an unquestionable and unquestioned expression of reality cannot be found within that ideology. In addition, the ideology requires the creation of that level of discourse to conceal its nature as ideological. In efforts to hide the true nature of ideologies, we often find open, ideological arguments that compete with literary themes. It is readily apparent that such arguments have a different

function. We shall not discuss this here. The important point to note is that
the consequence of our argument is that an ideology is always a kind of
mythology. In our modern societies, where ideologies are more transparent than
in primitive societies, literature is more *sui generis* and autonomous as a counterpart and in counterpoint. As people believe less and less in ideologies, literature
takes over more and more as a specific way of handling one's problems with
the real. In so-called primitive societies, on the other hand, ideology and literature are one and the same.

5.4. *Fiction and reality*

Let us now suppose that a given problem arises and is recognized as raising
a question about an idea for a given ideological system. It cannot be treated as
a problem within the thought system in question. It must be rhetoricized
through some form of mediation. A solution has to be found that indirectly
implies or suggests the validity of a preconceived idea through ideological
causality.

The original problem cannot be directly dealt with in terms of the ideology
involved. The initial question must be displaced by another question whose
answer can be found directly or indirectly (by inference) in the ideology. However, such an answer is only a *fiction* since the original problem is repressed
and then dissembled under the guise of another problem which means to adequately express the original problem but actually differs from it. If the job
is done correctly, illusion ensues. What is *fictionalized* in such a displacement
is the initial question. When an immanent problematic that expresses another
problematic is unfolded, fiction is created. Fiction is then an illustration of
the rhetoric of ideology. But the natural consequence of the process of fictionalization is that the ideological problem[28] disappears into the new and
different problem that conceals it. The discourse that emerges is not ideological
stricto sensu even if it is an ideological response. The ideological effect of an
ideological problem is a non-ideological solution (politically speaking at least):
the problematological answer to the ideological problem is another question that
is not *directly*, that is, *literally*, ideological. The fictionality of fiction, that
which characterizes fiction as fiction, is not strictly speaking ideological. Hence
literariness generally evokes human emotions or aesthetic pleasure rather than
feelings associated with politics or legitimation of a social order. Literature is
ideological whereas literariness is simply poeticity and thus non-ideological.

To a certain extent, literature creates its own problems by making itself autonomous with respect to the problems that initially gave birth to it as a *sui generis* mode of discursivity, i.e. as fiction. It is rhetorically implied by some ideology *stricto sensu* and forms part of the ideology *lato sensu*. As textuality enables language users to create ideological *effects* according to the very nature of ideology, texts, so *fictionalized,* are only possible because of the *rhetoric* of ideology *stricto sensu*. Fiction emerges as the unfolding of a derivative problematic that displaces and conceals some original problematic. This is the core of the rhetoric of ideology: expression through concealment, in one word, displacement (*Verschiebung*). By displacing the problems it is supposed to answer, by actually duplicating them in *sui generis* forms it has to invent (*poiesis*), literature provides not an apocritical answer to the (ideological) problems in question but rather a problematological one. Literature is bound to refer to a problematic of its own and create or reveal new alternatives immanent in the text. Autonomous with regard to the problems from which it originates, literature escapes the limitations of time period in which these problems occurred.

Ambivalence is the key word when we consider the relationship between fiction and reality. This notion raises the general problem of real-ism and real-ity in fiction. Reality is *the* problem for ideologies in both their *stricto sensu and lato sensu* materializations. A question that must be rhetoricized is necessarily a question that falls outside the limits of a supposedly all-embracing thought system. Therefore, it is not a thought nor an idea, but instead, something pertaining to reality in the traditional sense of the word (since ideologies are also real, though in some other sense of the word). A problem that gives rise to a literary solution as a mediating factor between reality and ideology in order to render the two homogeneous is a question that cannot directly be assimilated to the ideology *in question*; hence fiction, or more specifically, the fictionalization of the question is necessary. The question to be fictionalized remains outside the ideology which must nonetheless handle it. In its particularity, the question will receive a particularized literary solution, but it will not be given a literary treatment as a question addressing the real as real, since the real remains a question for us. By definition, reality cannot be assimilated within a thought system except figuratively: as reality, it is bound to remain external since reality is precisely externality.

The ideological problem *stricto sensu* must be considered as solved and, at the same time, as unproblematic, i.e. as having never raised any question. This is a fiction, of course. But if we look behind the curtains of fiction, we discover that this double requirement can only be met *with ambivalence* with respect to the problem. This notion simply means that the problem remains posed in spite of, or rather, because of its literary solution. Literature, then, transforms reality.

Who can really tell whether the prehistoric paintings on walls are due to unsuccessful hunts or to successful ones? Do the paintings result from the wish to thank the gods for having solved the tribe's problem of finding food or from the wish to tame the gods for not having solved this problem?

Epic novels of the middle ages raise similar questions. Let us consider the example of King Arthur and the knights of the Round Table. King Arthur is a model for all the knights. But such a model is ambivalent:[29] should this fictional king serve as an example of what monarchy ought to be like, or is it rather an apologia of monarchy *per se*? Is Chrétien de Troyes in favor of monarchy or against it? Is monarchy a good institution or a bad one? The question whether monarchy was good or bad presents a real dilemma, because, as Köhler explains, strong feudal lords were inclined to see King Arthur's story as a criticism leveled against a king who only maintains his position as more than just a feudal lord by restricting the lords' own power. On the other hand, a strong king could also favor such 'novels' since King Arthur illustrates the good effects of monarchy in the world of feudalism and the necessity of having a strong king to maintain peace and justice. Obviously, if the king is strong, it can only be at the expense of his vassals, and vice versa.

A last example. Is Don Quixote insane, as it is often stated in Cervantès, or is it rather the world in which he lives that is insane? Don Quixote exhibits odd behavior, but we are never told whether the peculiarity of his conduct is intrinsic to his nature or to the new values of the world in which knightly behavior inevitably creates the impression of being out of place. If Don Quixote were merely insane, would his adventures make sense at all? Is it Don Quixote who is ridiculous or the people and the events he must face?

In all these examples, we face a narrative structure in which the problem of reality is represented as solved and, at the same time, is suppressed. And we might ask ourselves whether the reality that is represented in the fiction is real or only fictional? Reality as a problem is rhetorically solved: fiction does not really offer an answer because reality can only be rhetorically handled even if we do not know what the *a priori* solution is.

What these examples reveal is the following:

(a) The residue left out of fiction as problematic is not the whole question but only what concerns reality as such. Thus the distinction between what is real and what is fictional within the text itself is somewhat blurred with the effect of increasing belief in the world of the text.

(b) Reality remains in its essential and infinitely diverse nature outside the realm of thought. It poses problems that are bound to remain at least partially unsolved since these problems are only treated in their bearing on ideology.

(c) After all, the main objective of fictionalization is to homogenize reality and ideology. This homogenization does not render the real ideal or abstract. What remains in question after fictionalization no longer presents a problem. Mediation trans-forms real question into a rhetorical one in terms of a body of ready-made answers. Mediation is therefore the form-alization of some initial problem through a discourse (i.e. a problematic), a process that expresses the problem in terms of the discourse. It is a translation into *fiction*. Mediation makes a real question homogeneous with the rhetorical questions embodied in a thought system. It enables the thought system to have an ideological bearing *stricto sensu* upon reality, i.e. to capture reality by generating an ideological justification and interpretation of what there is. Fiction has received an ideological determination that makes it, strictly speaking, dialectically unideological. Fiction always deals with reality. A problem is fictionalized only if it is external to a given thought system. The externality of the problem contradicts the definition of an ideology as universal. It challenges the given ideology since it testifies to the existence of an area of concern not encompassed by a supposedly all-embracing thought system. Fiction suppresses this contradiction by displacing the problem to another level of thought where the problem and its solution can be made homogeneous and treated discursively (where it becomes possible to find a solution for the problem that is compatible with the ideology). Fiction, then, represents reality even if it does so on a figurative level. Literature is ideological discourse from which all directly ideological elements have been removed. As a result, it opens up new problematic areas. Being autonomous with respect to the immediate reality from which it originated, a literary solution can be qualified as *unreal*, that is, as *fictional* even if, in the last analysis, it does address itself to reality.

Viewed as a literary solution to a real question, fiction embodies both a question and its answer. However, from an ideological point of view, the *real* remains in its non-ideological aspects irreducibly real and fiction refers back to an original problem that is different from the one it fictionally addresses. Fiction only provides a 'false solution' to the original problem by displacing it to another level of discursivity that is specifically erected to eliminate the problem as a real problem. The reality now expressed fictionally is no longer ideological.

Fiction is *poiesis* since it must represent ideological problems through other questions. These new problems are immanent in the textuality of the text. They are auto-contextualized by the text as an intrinsic feature of a litarery text. The rhetoric through which textuality comes into being, i.e. style or form, is characterized by that necessity of auto-contextualization that we do not find with other texts. Since the problems directly treated in non-literary texts are not immanent in them but come from some external context and are directly dealt with, the more non-linguistic information that can be presupposed in everyday life must be *directly* expressed in literary uses of language. This, I think, constitutes what will always be the difference between a police report and a detective story, however realistic a story may seem to be or however elegantly the police report may be written.

Let us now summarize. Literature, in fact, suppresses the problem of the real world that gave birth to it by fictionalizing the problem: fiction is the solution to some ideological quandary met with in the real world. When reality is negated, fiction necessarily ensues. When the original problem is fictionalized, it is translated and transfigured. Since the literary solution evades the *real* problem, its solution must be *fictional* though it is indirectly related to and deals with reality. Thus, even when it is meant to distance itself from ideology, fiction always has a bearing upon reality and can thereby address readers over a gap of centuries.

The literary solution does not appear *as a solution* because its displacing function guarantees its autonomy with respect to the problem from which it originated. Nonetheless, the literary solution is the problematological expression of a certain relationship to reality. We must remember that ideological problems are not deficiencies at all; they simply represent questions raised by an ideology's relationship to the world.

In literature, ideological problems are expressed through different problems that fiction bases on the original problems. Technically and stylistically, the representation of the original question takes place as the fictional problematic unfolds, short of being engrafted at the conclusion as in detective stories. Reality is then *figured out*, that is, figuratively dealt with. In some cases, fiction endeavors to provide a credible version of a situation that is not normally expressed. In other cases, the presentation of the problem is so enigmatic that it *ipso facto* distances the reader from reality, thus making it more likely that he will enter into *fiction* so created. In all cases, a problem is represented fictionally; the illusion of reality is created or a new relationship with reality is established through fiction. The necessity for fiction *qua* fiction to relate to reality reflects the greater necessity that fiction address a real problem. However indirectly and figuratively a real problem is treated through fiction, a real problematic is unfolded and is expressed by fictional means; reality is depicted through fiction, although such a depiction can at times be quite abstract.

The question that displaces the original problem reflects, in some very loose sense of the word. reality. According to the problematological conception of language, referentiality is an essential feature of language use, and the ways in which the references are denoted are many. In fiction, reality is actually translated twice. First, the problematological displacement enables the ideological aspects of the interpretation of the real to be de-ideologized and represented neutrally to create a derived ideological effect. Second, the fictionalization of the original problem gives rise to a new question that does not directly concern ideology and that reflects or expresses a reality of its own. This fictionalization figures out some specific (i.e. non-political) ideas and represents them in a fictional, but quite *sui generis* manner. This is *poiesis*. Textuality raises many questions, and it is not necessarily *the* question of meaning that is of primary concern.

In other words, aspects of reality are figured out in fiction. The ideas embodied in fiction may be understood ideologically *stricto sensu*. But, at the same time, the questions raised by fiction are ideologically neutral. The text, i.e. the literary solution, then appears to be devoid of any ideological function. A fictional text is made up of answers that are not expressed as answers, although that is what they literally are. On the other hand, the questions such answers evoke are *generally speaking* ideological: many ideas are suggested concerning the reality represented, and these are meant to enable us to grasp it as such. By representation, we do *not* mean a literal reproduction or picture of the real but a way of treating a problem, one that implies underlying or manifest referential interrogatives.

As autonomous units, literary texts put forth new questions and, consequently, figuratively imply new ideas apart from and resulting from the ideological ones that are also implied. The autonomization of literature as an ideological response causes the emergence of de-ideologized ideas which underlie literature and contribute to its meaning.

Fiction enables us to see things from a different point of view and to understand what is going on inside or outside of our minds. However, such an understanding results from a second-level (or reflexive) reading where ideas are thematically grasped and rearranged consistently into an apocritically formulated problematic. The original problem raised by an ideology's confrontation with the external world is captured through literature and this solution may give rise to a new frame of reference. The real problem that is immanent in the fiction and meant to provide an illustration of or, on the other hand, an uncriticizable criticism of an ideology offers a figurative view of the reality to be captured. This illustration is literally representative of *something* in question and literarily figurative of something which is fictionally in question.

5.5. *Literary forms as means of materializing the problematological difference*

Fiction deals with its own internal problematic. The whole question is how it does this. The key to the answer is the problematological difference. Literary forms are meant to embody this difference. The range of different literary forms result from the different ways in which the difference is materialized; the use of stylistic forms is grounded in the exigency of the problematological difference. The specificity of these forms rests upon the specificity of literariness. Then, form is nothing but the way in which a fictionalization of the problems in question is achieved. Form is the mode of representation of a given problem with respect to the problematological difference. Fiction does not aim to represent the problems of reality but rather to represent a problematic of its own. The representation of this problematic, in turn, reveals a new reality or a new way of seeing reality. Reality is represented only indirectly, as becomes more and more apparent the farther we move from mimetic prose and the closer we come to poetry or problematic texts, which, in some sense, also describe the real.

What is the General Law of the use of forms in fiction? It can be formulated in various ways but always with the same implication. Fiction creates its own rhetorical procedures according to the following rule:

The more a problem is expressed literally, the less the form counts as the means to mark the difference between what is problematological and what is the solution, since this is made clear in the text. The less literally or the more figuratively a problem is expressed, the more problematic the whole textuality is in comparison to habitual discourse. The more a text is figurative of a problem, the more the literal sense of the text (mimesis) suggests at least one non-literal reading expressive of the text's problematic. The more a text is problematic in itself, as a text, the more the text deconstructs literal reading and the dichotomy between the literal and the non-literal, the univocal and the plurality of equi-plausible interpretations, tends to vanish. When a problem is explicitly stipulated in the literary solution, the problematological difference is textually marked. Textuality is the means by which the progress from problem to solution is achieved. Form plays a minor role. We are close to everyday language. References to the world of the reader are more immediate and there is a kind of natural pragmatics of reading involved here. When the problem is not explicitly marked in the literary text itself, the latter must somehow establish the difference. Symbols are used as textual riddles which can only be solved as the level of the text as a whole. A greater problematicity of those symbols increases the difficulty to make a distinction between literal and figurative readings, which is itself a dichotomy that is meant to mark the problematological difference. Textuality becomes itself the 'meaning' of the riddles involved in figural language, which does not refer any longer to something other than its own unfolding. De-pragmatization ensues and second-level and non-progressive reading are then necessary.

Or:

The more a problem dealt with through literature is expressed literally, the closer its literal expression will come to our habitual and everyday mode of speech. Auto-contextualization makes a text fictional. This can only be achieved by means of rhetorical devices. This process of auto-contextualization of problems, more than the employment of figural language, characterizes fiction and literature and can also come about with habitual and non-figurative language. What is figured out in any text is what it means. Such meaning is not literally *said* as being so-and-so.

In other terms, when the problem treated in a text is specified, we also know *what* is described in the text; we can perceive the unfolding of the text's problematic, that is, its resolution. Reality is then represented within the text. Fiction stems from the necessity of expressing the problem and the solution through a language as close to *reality* as possible. But, as the above rule implies, *realism* is not a necessity since a particular form or style is not essential. Fairy tales, for instance, confront the reader with problems that the tales were meant to resolve; the solutions offered are sometimes magical. Use of habitual language in literature does not mean realism: it simply means that the mode of arranging sentences and terms is borrowed from the non-fictional realm of everyday linguistic practice. The interest represented by the problematic and its apocritical unfolding captures the reader, i.e. leads him to the 'willing suspension of disbelief'.

The less a problem is explicitly described, the more it must be suggested. Suggestion can only be achieved through stylistic procedures, the so-called rhetorical devices or tropes. A metaphor, for instance, as Aristotle showed, is an enigma since it is literally meaningless.

The less a problem is specifically affirmed, the greater the risk of problematological confusion or, here, non-differentiation between the text as an entity and its literal components, i.e. the sentences it contains. Literally, the sentences say *something* which is used to suggest *something else*: reference becomes a sign and ceases to be an end in itself. The textuality of the text is then unlikely to refer realistically to the real. In other words, reality is suggested rather than directly referred to. Texts formally ask for some other proposition or discourse and refer *back* to the question they answer, not by stating it but by suggesting it. Referentiality, or *mimesis*, becomes a tool for *semiosis*; the literal reading of the text constitutes a code. Poetry is a good example of such a rhetorical procedure. Enigmatic textuality can be created by metaphors, explicit questions that refer to a more global, though unstipulated problem, rhymes, and other stylistic arrangements alien to the *everyday forms* of language.

Thus the less explicit a problem is, the more the textual answers must refer back to it non-literally. In all cases, the text must always refer back to the problem(s) it answers in some way or other.

From the hermeneutical point of view, we can say that the *poiesis* of suggestion renders the text all the more enigmatic, since *what* is 'said' is not really *said*. The more enigmatic a text is, the more a second-level or reflexive reading leading to a consistent interpretation becomes necessary. The less enigmatic a text is, the more the problem is expressed literally and therefore the more such a reflexive reading becomes superfluous.

5.6. *The birth of the novel: Don Quixote as an illustration*

The novel, according to Bakhtin (1978), is a *sui generis* rhetorical procedure. As such, the novel is linked to a specific time period that rendered it possible if not necessary as a literary genre after the death of the epic.

Rhetorically speaking, the novel is undoubtedly a new rhetorical form. Bakhtin sees it as the linguistic expression of a dialogical structure between the author and the narrator. From a linguistic point of view, the novel embodies an attitude of self-questioning, whatever happens to its various characters and whatever they do. A novel is characterized by the fact that its speaker is in question. Self-questioning by some individual involves an increase in the role granted to subjectivity and to its synthetic-active mode of being-in-the-world. The novel separates the contemplative author from the action of the story, which is represented as a dialogical and internal dimension of the narration. Since problems are explicitly internalized in the novel, forms play a lesser role and a multiplicity of linguistic practices can compose the novel as a literary genre. As a result, the novel is closer to everyday use of language than are any other traditional literary genres.

Studying the novel from the point of view of its history, specialists have come to realize more and more that the novel is intrinsically the embodiment of questions. The epic had already been defined in terms of a quest:

"La société occidentale est la seule à avoir produit le roman, parce que, seule, elle a préféré au rite à l'aventure." (Laurent 1977: 64)

The novel is probably due to the rise of the individual and to the breakdown of traditional social units. When we examine the gradual evolution of literature that led to the emergence of the novel, we are confronted with a series of books that present their heroes as having a progressively more individualistic outlook:

"Ces livres supposent des sociétés desserrées dont chaque membre se heurte à des questions et n'attend la réponse que de lui-même. Il faut ce flou pour que le roman naisse, ou renaisse." (Laurent 1977: 59)

In other words, society, and reality in general, raise more and more questions in a world where social ties become ever looser and are emptied of their past significance and legitimacy. Thus, as Laurent (1977: 59, 64) puts it: "A novel is always insoluble", "Change is reality itself and marginality is the rule" (translation mine).

Georg Lukács, more than any other theoretician, associated literature with problematicity. The Greeks did not react to reality as if it represented an unbridgeable gap between the individual and the world. They compensated for an incipient distantiation with something other than ancient mythemes, which were deemed inadequate and less and less applicable to evolving reality.

"The Greek knew only answers but no questions, only solutions (even if enigmatic ones) but no riddles, only forms but no chaos." (Lukács 1978: 31)

With the growth of the individual and the loosening of social ties, the dominant literary form became increasingly concerned with individual deeds. But the significance of these deeds remained expressed in terms of a social quest of a world where life *has* a meaning that may not yet have been found but that is globally unquestioned. As for the novel,

"[it] is the epic of an age in which the extensive totality of life is no longer direct-ly given, in which the immanence of meaning in life has become a problem . . . The epic gives form to a totality of life that it rounded from within; the novel seeks, by giving form, to uncover and construct the concealed totality of life . . . Thus, the fundamental form-determining intention of the novel is objectivised as the psychol-ogy of the novel's heroes: they are seekers." (Lukács 1978: 55-60)[30]

In other words, there is a specific relationship between the hero and its world in the novel. The epic expresses some kind of harmony through lyrical forms such as verses or drama and thus forms a structure of contemplative discursivity that can compensate for the lost individual and even give meaning to such a loss. In the novel, the hero is an individual who constructs the real for and by himself. Quite often, the author identifies himself with this individual by using the *I* of the first-person narrator. The relationship between man and the world is not resolved at some level of rhetorical lyricism where harmony is formally created. Instead, the hero must create a world of his own where he can feel at home as if nothing existed independent of or outside his construction.

This explains why *Robinson Crusoe* and *Don Quixote* are often considered as the first novels. In both works, reality is not taken for granted but, instead, questioned. The protagonists must solve questions and must do it alone. Robin-son Crusoe, for instance, is not merely metaphorically individualized but he is also physically so. He *has* to build a world with his own hands and his own mind. In this sense, Robinson Crusoe is the symbol of the new man emerging out of the old society: he is the individual *par excellence.* But as Marthe Robert so nicely puts it, Crusoe is nonetheless the son of the Quixote, a son better adapted to the world than his father, who was seen as insane in a world that was not yet ready for the quest of the individual.

"Donquichottesque, en effet, Robinson l'est dans toutes les couches de son person-nage d'homme errant et de solitaire invétéré." (Robert 1976: 176)

In fact, Crusoe, more than any other literary character represents the indi-vidual who 'starts from scratch' without the weight of a past that would render him unfit for the new times. He symbolizes a new beginning, even though this beginning is indirectly presented amid circumstances very far from those of England.

Don Quixote, however, is really the first novel. Picaresque 'novels' take reality for granted, however adverse and inimical it may be. The heroes of these novels try to survive in a pre-established world. However, unlike these heroes, Don Quixote has to question the world he lives in in order to find (or lose) himself as the Erring Knight. As Ortega y Gasset (1981: 99) said, "en el nuevo order de las cosas las aventuras son imposibles"; the *picaro* was the last 'adventurer'. Don Quixote symbolizes the inadequacy of the individual in a changing world. Don Quixote's adventures symbolize the loneliness of man in a reality that can no longer be taken for granted; he thereby reflects questioning addressed to a changed world, a questioning that is actually self-questioning verging on madness. Only ideas remain and ideas that lack a corresponding reality become inadequate: Don Quixote is seized by an obsession that like all extreme fixations is bound to lead to failure. If the Greeks knew only answers and lacked the questions, Don Quixote only knows the question and never finds its answer. He is literature becoming a question.

Let us now examine the book in more detail. In *Don Quixote*, literature treats of literature in a masterly way. The role and function of literature, its uses, misuses and abuses, are among the main themes of the work: *Don Quixote* is a literary text concerned with the problems raised by literary texts, their authors, their readers, and perhaps, most importantly, the relationship between literature and ideology.

The world has changed, but Don Quixote still believes it conforms to what he read of it in books of chivalry. Buried in the literature of an age long past, he fails to see how much the real world has changed. He has progressively lost contact with reality, and when he finally cleaves to his old books to live the life of an knight errant in quest of adventures, he does not see that he belongs to a world where knights are an irretrievable part of the vanished past. He refuses to see that *his* world is no longer governed by the laws of chivalry. Hence, Don Quixote becomes a ridiculous character and we find his conduct just as humorous as the characters he encounters in his adventures do. The ludicrous aspect of Don Quixote's attitude towards the world and to his misfortunes stems from the fact that he rejects reality since it does not conform to what he has read in the books. Don Quixote sees the world in terms of the vision contained in his beloved stories. When there is a gap between the two worlds, he bridges it by explaining it in terms of magical forces like those at work in the stories he reads. Reality becomes an illusion that can be accounted for by magic, the very same magic that we find in books of chivalry. Don Quixote thereby re-establishes the *a priori* reality that conforms to the basic views expounded in his books.

What does this have to do with literature and ideology? At first reading, apparently nothing, but upon a closer study, the novel is seen to *express the very relationship* between literature and ideology that we are concerned with. The essential feature of ideology is its closure. No challenge can rationally be made against it. In fact, ideology is as closed upon itself as Don Quixote's own (mental) world is. As Sancho Panza's efforts show, no rational argument against Don Quixote's beliefs can be successful or convincing. The most famous example of this is Don Quixote's attack on the windmills, which the erring knight takes for monstrous giants.

> " 'O, my goodness!' cried Sancho, 'Didn't I tell your lordship to look what you were doing, for they were only windmills? Nobody could mistake them, unless he had, windmills on the brain.'
> 'Silence, friend Sancho', replied Don Quixote, 'Matters of wars are more subject than most to continual change. What is more, I think, *and that is the truth*, that the same sage Friston who rabbled me of my room and my books has turned these giants into windmills, to cheat me of the glory of conquering them.' " (Cervantes 1950:I, 69; emphasis mine)[31]

The striking fact here is that, whatever happens, Don Quixote is always right in his own eyes. Not only can nothing really change his point of view, but he also conceives of everything that seems to prove his vision of the world false as a corroboration of this vision. In other words, since Don Quixote effectively excludes all possibilities of his views being disproved, no question can arise about these beliefs that cannot be answered by them. The questions that could be posed and that Sancho actually raises are then what we call *rhetorical questions. Don Quixote* expresses the rhetoricalness of literature and its role as a mediator. Don Quixote is a caricature because he appears as merely idea; he completely presents mediatization all by himself. Questions can only serve as a pretext for confirming beliefs previously and independently held. How could those questions be adequately and effectively posed, if not literarily? Cervantes' work does not much illustrate the ludicrousness of someone who reads too much and lives too little as it shows how ridiculous a man can be when he adheres to a closed system of thoughts that nothing and nobody can successfully challenge. What Cervantes wants us to laugh at is the ridiculousness of the Quixote's behavior, a behavior that can only be denounced through literature. The ideology of the past is contained in and symbolized by the books of chivalry.

The negative aspects of the character of Don Quixote — the fact that he appears ridiculous — conceals a positive reading, namely that *we* are *all* ridiculous when we cling to an ideology despite the existence of facts that contradict its ideas. Since ideology cannot be formulated literally, the best way to illustrate its absurdity is through a story in which a character behaves with stupidity though in perfect conformity with the dictates of ideology. *Don Quixote* exemplifies the role of literature with respect to ideologies, by expressing through illustration what cannot be stated explicitly and literally. Any description of how an ideology functions would involve ideology. The real questions that an ideology is unable to face in a literal discussion but must instead treat rhetorically are the specific subject matter of literature, and *it is this very fact* that the *Don Quixote* exemplifies. Don Quixote represents ideological closure and the impossibility of transgressing it. The character of Don Quixote points to the fact that literature is the only means of successfully challenging ideology: Cervantes' work shows how an ideological closure can be unveiled as being ideological and hence inadequate. This enables the reader to call into question that which does not allow any questions except the rhetorical ones (to which the ideology in question has all the answers). An ideological system 'rhetoricalizes' questions raised against it, while literature keeps them alive as representations of real questions and makes them impervious to 'rhetoricalization'. In other words, Cervantes' achievement was to demonstrate the use of literature to attack ideology. But the character of Cervantes' hero is fundamentally ambiguous. What literature can and should do is the main *idea* expressed by *Don Quixote*. This is the positive side of Cervantes' poor hero. After all, he defends widows and orphans even if he does it in the name of an outdated and somewhat comic ideology. This ideology claims, like all others, to rely on universal values and high moral standards that are not respected in the real world. Typical of this positive attitude is the episode described in the fourth chapter in which Don Quixote comes to the rescue of a poor shepherd boy who has been beaten by his master who had also refused to pay him. The striking point in this episode is that, while apparently complying with Don Quixote's order to release and pay the boy, the countryman, once left alone again with the boy, beats him harder than ever and finally leaves him nearly dead.

"But at least he untied him and gave him leave to go and look for his judge to execute the sentence he had pronounced. Andrew set off in a fury, swearing to go and find the valorous Don Quixote de la Mancha and tell him exactly what had happened. Then his master would have to pay him sevenfold. But for all that, he wept as he went, and his master remained behind laughing; and thus did the valorous Don Quixote redress that wrong." (Cervantes 1950: I, 50)

In this paragraph, we see the extent of the intellectual's vanity concerning the influence of his actions upon society. However, even if the intellectual – he who reads books and wishes to enforce justice accordingly – plays a futile game and fights windmills, and if he, unlike Don Quixote, realizes the absurdity of his struggle, it is unclear if other choices remain open to him. Must he refrain from protesting when the highest values of mankind are trodden upon? Reading Cervantes, we are forced to realize how ridiculous and pointless Don Quixote's struggle is[32] and to ask who will publically defend the universal values that are constantly neglected in favor of particular interests if the intellectual does not do so. Who will speak in favor of those who dare not speak? Maybe the intellectual reads too many books, and maybe literature leads him along the garden path of 'chivalric deeds' that consists of fighting battles that are already lost, but surely this is preferable to condoning or siding with those who primarily cherish personal interests and only enter into battles they can win. Herein lies the absurdity and futility of the intellectual: who wants to fight a battle that he knows is already lost, just for the sake of moral principles? This, at least, is the view of those who would never embark upon such campaigns.

This discussion can shed light upon the ambiguity in the character of Don Quixote. He is simultaneously seen as being comic and tragic, as acting out of a sense of duty and following his whim, as being laughable and extremely serious. He is both someone we would not want to be and an example that should inspire us in our moral conduct. Hence the story of the erring knight and his windmills represents the odyssey of all self-conscious intellectuals, while at the same time, it makes the intellectuals aware of the vanity of their vanity – sorry – of *our* vanity. Cervantes' masterpiece endeavors to present someone who is ridiculous because of having read and believed too many books and who, in spite of that and because of it, is also a man of great virtue and a true knight. *Don Quixote* is also the story of someone who refuses to abandon a closed system of beliefs, and who, therefore, is completey out of touch with the real world; our erring knight, then, also represents the absurdity of all those who cling to beliefs out of complacency and refuse to listen to those who do not share the same beliefs or to see the facts that contradict their ideas. This tension between the positive and negative aspects of Don Quixote's character is necessary since systems of beliefs always become closed, although they each claim, even through their most dogmatic aspects, to defend the essential values of mankind. This tension between an alleged universality and a real particularity can only be expressed literarily if one wishes to avoid ending in dogmatism.

Now let us turn to the problem of the ambiguous nature of ideology. Just as it is both pointless and necessary to oppose injustice, it is both futile and necessary to fight bad ideas. As suggested by Cervantes' *Don Quixote*, literature serves the double purpose of showing us what ideology does, can do, and should do, and revealing what it cannot accomplish. A writer is like the erring knight: he fights the windmills, and even when he accepts some prevailing ideology, he must remember that he is still deceiving himself if he takes himself too seriously. Nonetheless, the intellectual is useful, if only by criticizing people in power. Intellectuals and writers, from Socrates to Neruda, would not have been persecuted, if their voices had never been heard. However vain the intellectuals' protest may sound, it is already too much noise for those who resent all types of protest. And this is enough to make the utmost futility a little less futile.

5.7. *Conclusion*

Literature is defined as fiction. Fiction consists of several interrelated dimensions; literature is therefore a specific mode of discourse.

(a) Fictional discourse is the problematological displacement of reality as it is particularized in the form of specific questions. The real is represented fictionally via other ideas which enable us to conceive it as such in its particularization. Fiction is not opposed to reality; it is merely a way of representing and of relating to it. However, fiction does not directly solve the problem(s) posed by reality; a fictional solution is achieved by transforming the real problems into invented ones that are meant to express them.

(b) From the point of view of linguistic technique, fiction is a use of language that auto-contextualizes problems in a way that everyday discourse does not. Fiction approaches problems in a manner unlike that of everyday speech. Here fiction is equated with *poiesis*. *Poiesis* is a movement by virtue of which a given problem is treated textually. Fiction is a particular way of formalizing a question, i.e., it is *style*. Style is a dynamic rhetoric resulting in a text that embodies and *formally* expresses the problematological difference. *Fiction is a* question-answer relationship marked through textual *form(s)* only (i.e. through a problematological difference).

(c) Fiction captures the reader's attention by temporarily freeing him from everyday and hence real problems. If the reader finds a solution in some literary discourse, the solution can only be fictional since the adequate resolution to a real problem must take place at the level of reality. Aesthetic pleasure is generated when we feel we have found a solution to our problems in fiction. Thus, when fiction succeeds in releasing us from our problems, it solves them in a certain sense by giving us a sensation of aesthetic pleasure. To do this, literature displaces real problems by turning them into figurative ones that indirectly represent them. A fictional text, like any other text, questions the reader; but unlike other texts, the questions are treated indirectly. Some derived staging of our problems is offered which does not directly commit us to face the devastating problem that we *are;* we are bound to remain an unsolved question till the end of our lives in virtue of the mere fact that we exist. Fiction addresses itself to all of us and calls us into question through the mediation of ideas which are not literally expressed. We are thereby indirectly, i.e. through some particular case, committed to something which speaks to us universally. This universality is, of course, a concrete one since it is a common feature between *me* as a particular person and another particular situation or person.

Fiction, then, is *mimesis* or representation, *poiesis* or rhetorical invention of textuality, and a psychoanalytical answer.

(d) The law of *symbolic weakening* governs the formation of literary genres: the more a problem is literally expressed, the less it needs to be made distinct from its solution at a symbolical level. If the problem is not literally expressed in the text, it must nonetheless be expressed and this can only be done indirectly or symbolically.

This law implies that references are less likely to be employed to mark the problem a text deals with; instead, the problem remains implicit in the text; references serve as 'signifiers' with respect to something other than what they literally represent. The text's references act as a code for the problem; what is ultimately referred to is what is symbolized by the normal references of the words contained in the text.

A problem can always be very enigmatically specified *within* a text, or stated without referring to its corresponding solution. This fact does not contradict the law of the forms in fiction since the problematological difference is still respected.

(e) Ideology is always concealed in the forms of fiction. Whether the problem dealt with in fiction is actually *specified* or merely suggested, the relationship is never expressed. In the latter case, because problems are suggested, in the former, because problems are explicit and non-ideological either. The forms of fiction never betray their underlying ideological structure, or, for it amounts to the same thing, we can also say that they always reveal it.

6. THE INTERPRETATIVE PROCESS

6.1. *Beyond traditions and omissions*

Neither the continental tradition in philosophy nor its analytically oriented counterpart have devoted much attention to the interpretative process.

Most linguists and philosophers of language have dissociated the analysis of meaning from the analysis of interpretation, the process of discovering meaning. Their reason is mainly that in literary criticism, as in science, discovery is an unimportant phenomenon. The study of this discovering process is not supposed to contribute significantly towards the understanding of linguistic or scientific phenomena, because interpretation is a psychological process, not a philosophical one. Two different 'views' of the process of interpretation have been advanced. One holds that the process of understanding takes place inside of language while the other holds that it occurs outside of it. By 'inside of language', we mean that the structure of the propositions composing a work and the relationships between them are the sole source of the discovery of meaning, and that interpretation consists of the production of new propositions equivalent to the original ones. Interpretation, then, is a quasi-mechanical process based on analyzing (recognizing?, evaluating?) the structure of language with or without the aid of a principle. When we say that interpretation occurs 'outside of language', we conceive of interpretation as a psychological and/or intuitive process not dependent on linguistic structure. Such a process, by definition, cannot be objectively characterized and is not related to *language* use or the study of language. In both cases, the consequences of the process are the same: meaning presents itself either automatically through some kind of inner and quasi-mechanical generative procedure which results *in* language or, psychologically, through a skill which cannot be objectively characterized. In the one case, meaning is acquired by revelation or by some intrinsic automatism[33] that we possess in virtue of our being capable of language use. In the second case, we arrive at meaning through some kind of intuition. The important fact is that both cases presuppose a conception of language that justifies ignoring the importance of meaning *discovery* in the analysis of *meaning*. Such disregard for interpretation rests upon the dissociation of meaning and its discovery, and reveals much about contemporary views of language, more particularly, the adequacy – or inadequacy – of their conceptions of meaning. We sense that a fully developed theory of meaning must be complemented by an explanation of the process of understanding. The fact that a theory of language deems such a requirement unnecessary is sufficient to show that the theory is theoretically incomplete and unsatisfactory.

Conceptions of language that imply the dissociation mentioned above are all of the same type. They are characterized by the notion of self-sufficiency, i.e. that propositions are self-sufficient units. A quasi-autonomous view of language, for instance, renders the acquisition peripheral and dependent upon context and subjectivity; or worse, understanding is conceived of as being an inner, if not autonomical, fact of language. The propositional theory of meaning can be counted among the views of language that enable theoreticians to consider the process of understanding as unimportant. Frege's precept, for instance, is typical of the mechanical procedure involved in the inside-language view of meaning: it stipulates that we should substitute for each term an equi-referential term to obtain the meaning of the sentence that we wish to understand. By analytically repeating this procedure, as is done in mathematical demonstrations, we could then grasp the signification of whole texts. The adequate substitution can always be made in each text according to Frege's view of language. On the other hand, Wittgenstein considers the process of understanding as philosophically uninteresting since meaning remains a proposition, i.e. another piece of language. Here too, it is language that makes possible the process of its understanding. Wy should we even look for any *sui generis* mental procedure, as psychologists do, in contrast to linguists or philosophers, when such a procedure cannot be distinguished from its sentential manifestation and is just another type of sentence production? Would it even *matter* if both processes, the psychological and the logical one, could be distinguished?

It would be misleading, however, to affirm that the process whereby meaning is acquired has received no independent attention. The main concern of *hermeneutics* is, after all, interpretation as an independent phenomenon. Maybe we can object that the independence granted interpretation is too great. Indeed, hermeneutics has failed to offer any theory explaining the functioning of language to complement its theory of interpretation. We here see a situation opposite to that of the analytic tradition. In fact, hermeneutics had – or has – a different aim, one that justifies the lack of an articulate view of language in the eyes of its supporters. But we should not forget that *our* problem here is to establish such a continuity between the theory of language and the discovery of meaning and to develop a consistent theory of meaning *and* understanding.

The hermeneutical tradition has formulated several definitions of under-standing. This multiplicity of definitions has often led the opponents of hermeneutics to contend that the notion of interpretation is arbitrarily and subjectively defined and that hermeneutics is therefore deprived of any unity. Schleiermacher was especially concerned with religion and sacred texts that cannot be interpreted literally without appearing contradictory. Dilthey was interested in demarcating the human sciences from the other sciences, *Verstehen* and *Erklären*, which employ different methods. Gadamer envisions understanding as our relationship to the past, in terms of its cultural effects upon the present, whereas Betti sees in understanding a mere *method* for social sciences. Ricoeur believes that hermeneutics is related more specifically to language: its object of study is unconscious messages, metaphors, and other instances of what Heidegger defined as existential manifestations. Is understanding then the manifestation of our religious nature, a distinctive feature of mind, a *sui generis* method adopted by social sciences that does not *explain* but rather enables us to *comprehend* our relationship to the past and tradition in terms of effects (*Wirkungsgeschichte*), or is it something totally different?

Where do we find the unity in hermeneutics? *Symbol* is the key word. Symbols receive multiple readings (Ricoeur) that are related. Literal and unique interpretations are then avoided since this would totally destroy the symbols' content, as it is the case with religious texts (Schleiermacher). The explication of ambiguous symbols is one of the main concerns of the human sciences. After all each version given for a symbol is itself as much of a choice as its adoption in the first place (Heidegger). A symbol is then the expression of a value that needs to be interpreted because it has a social impact (Weber) in that it is a motive for action or judgment in a given *society*. Hermeneutics seeks to illuminate the process through which the indeterminacy that characterizes symbols can be mastered (Betti, Dilthey). Such a process of disambiguation is called understanding. It ascribes *a* meaning inherited from the past or reconstructed on the basis of what tradition has transmitted to us about that which is to be interpreted (Gadamer's *Überlieferung*), suggested by prejudices and ideologies, or conditioned by one's existential predicament (which, if we agree to follow Heidegger's philosophy of *Dasein* and human nature, enables us to bridge the gap between past and present).

Weber often employed interpretation to reconstruct the meanings of past societies that have become alien to us today. This enabled him to understand how these societies functioned, especially with reference to their systems of legitimation. The ambiguity that Weber had noticed stemmed from the fact that a set of beliefs or practices, whether abandonned by modern society or not, can mean various things and express different essential values to different people. Symbols are *historically* marked.

In sum, hermeneutics comes to the foreground when polysemy is recognized as a rule, and when symbolism is seen as more than a limited phenomenon in the use of linguistic signs. When there is a choice to be made that amounts to a disambiguation of what 'naturally' and inevitably can have several compatible and reasonable interpretations, hermeneutics has a role to play.

As we all know, such ambiguity pervades many areas of human experience, from the level of psychic mechanism, where symbols enable our unconscious to condense and displace disturbing information in such a way that this information does not threaten and even preserves the integrity of our ego, to religion. This explains why hermeneutics is often associated with the question 'What does it mean?' But, in cases of hermeneutical concern, the scope of this question is nonetheless more restricted than it might seem at first glance. The *it* in the question pertains to a quite specific range of objects, namely symbols, and, more precisely, to ambiguous symbols. Mathematicians would hardly turn to hermeneutics when they wish to understand some theorem or other. However, some theorists would deny that non-ambiguous symbols exist at all. Mathematicians explicitly render them univocal by ascribing only *one* interpretation to each. This is already a hermeneutical procedure of a sort; unlike other examples, the rules are already codified here. Polysemy is the rule, words in general have more than one meaning, and there are various ways through which language users eliminate inappropriate meanings and choose or define *the* one meaning they have in mind, in science as elsewhere. Hermeneutical procedures are therefore inherent in any use of language. Of more practical interest is the manner in which the framework of understanding is defined. What hermeneuticists wish to comprehend is how individuals or societies have effectively and actually understood culture and its symbols (texts, myths, existential attitudes, social values, and so forth) and especially how people of today understand the past's interpretation of culture and its symbols. To use the words of Gadamer, hermeneutics is preoccupied above all with *Wirkungsgeschichte*: the effects of the works of the past on our present understanding, on *our* relationship to tradition, insofar as this tradition affects our present. No wonder, then, that those hermeneuticists did not find it necessary to offer a theory of the *process* of understanding. They define the latter as the intellectual procedure by which one assimilates the past and merges it with the present. Hence, hermeneutics grants

great importance to *Überlieferung, Traditio*, etymologically that which is transmitted to us by the past. They act as if temporal and historical continuity
could give us the key to understanding how understanding functions at each
historical period and seem to believe that no new problem could ever arise that
tradition has not already solved. Philosophy, for instance, reduces itself to the
history of phylosophy *and* to the justification of this very thesis, a justification
which, if philosophical, must destroy itself. As a result,

> "understanding is not so much a method by means of which the enquiring mind
> approaches some selected object and turns it into objective knowledge, as some-
> thing of which a prior condition is its being situated within a process of tradition.
> Understanding itself proved to be an event, and the task of hermeneutics, seen
> philosophically, consists in asking what kind of understanding, what kind of science
> it is, that is itself changed by historical change." (Gadamer 1975a: 276)

Gadamer's basic query is 'What is understanding as a historically determined
phenomenon?' Gadamer submits understanding to tradition and sees it as a process of evolution of 'effects' upon future epochs. This Gadamerian question
is itself a manifestation of our contemporary understanding of understanding,
which sees understanding as always changing in form and content. Understanding is *our* relationship with the past. How it works here and now is secondary,
derivative, always limited to a particular time and space.

This conception can only leave us dissatisfied. Far be it from us to cast aside
historicity when interpretation is in question. How the works of the past
can speak to us today is an important question. But we have yet to determine
how understanding functions. We are surely not willing to content ourselves
with the assertion that understanding is variable and historically bound, and
that, as a result, it eludes a systematic theoretization. Rather, Gadamer's attitude seems to forbid us to seek for a *general* structure of understanding since
such an inquiry and its answer would be ahistorical. Nonetheless, understanding
is something and not just anything. Gadamer would object that, insofar as it
is, it *is* what it *has* always *been*: a fluctuating, 'epochal', phenomenon; history
taking account of itself in its general legacy of what was and remains.

This is perplexing, when we consider that we do not know more about
what understanding was in the past than about what it is now:

> "The hermeneutic phenomenon is basically not a problem of method at all. It is
> not concerned with a method of understanding, by means of which texts are sub-
> jected to scientific investigation like all other objects of experience." (Gadamer
> 1975a: xi)

It is little wonder, then, that Gadamer (1975b: 114) compared *Wirkungsge-schichte*, the 'historical effectiveness' of the past upon the present, to Hegel's absolute knowledge. *Wirkungsgeschichte* is itself an historical *moment* in the history of understanding. But all this does not help us render understanding more understandable. What is obviously lacking in the hermeneutic vision is a unified theory of interpretation, one that would include non-ambiguous language as well *and* would structure it within the same single theory of understanding: interpretation and language in both its ordinary and textual forms, whether ambiguous or univocal, should receive balanced treatment as much as should historicity. But, as Apel (1980: 84) reminds us, in the hermeneutic tradition, "the primary concern of hermeneutics was not *understanding the communicative understanding of the text by the contemporaries. It was rather understanding how the meaning of the texts can be understood by people of a later epoch by way of their historical understanding*".

The basic objections raised against recent hermeneutics in works like Gadamer (1975a) are the following:

(a) Everyday situations are not characterized by ambiguity, intrinsic or not. There is a difference between allegories or biblical sayings and a policeman's invective; the policeman's words usually lack the challenging symbolism we cherish in the works that we examine hermeneutically. But such everday situations are still interpreted by a hearer or reader and must be understood by him. They must be subject to the same theory of understanding as that explaining instances of ambiguous language.

(b) How should we proceed, and in fact how *do* we proceed, when we are confronted with several possible, compatible interpretations? How can we *rationally* proceed, if we agree to exclude intuition or revelation, to arrive at one interpretation and justify this choice, if we do not have some technique of understanding at our disposal? Intuition, revelation, and empathy are words which only cover modes of knowledge that elude all possible knowlegde.[34]

Not all speech situations are ambiguous; most of them are not. Even when they are, understanding remains an obscure process.

(c) A valid theory of interpretation cannot neglect language in the specific sense of the term, as it is understood within the analytic tradition. This is not a question of misplaced ecumenicalism but raher a basic requirement: for obvious reasons, hermeneutic structures must already exist at the level of language itself. If, for instance, we understand understanding as a questioning process, we still have to determine what questioning has to do with language and linguistic (or symbolic) objects. We can neither introduce nor presuppose a gap between understanding and what is understood as if the method used to deal with an object had nothing to do with the nature of the object itself. And if the method has *something* to do with its objects, then it is incumbent upon us to explain exactly what in the object determines the choice of the method used to study it.

We can now summarize what we require from an adequate theory of understanding:

(a) We need a rational description of meaning acquisition. The term 'rational' implies that no appeal be made to intuition, to the inner and inexpressible processes of the mind, or to revelation.

(b) An adequate theory of understanding must be applicable to *language* and to linguistic phenomena in general. This implies that we must go beyond the traditional boundaries of hermeneutics, i.e. the field's inquiries into religion, human existence, scientific methods, and so forth. It also implies that we must harmonize our theory of meaning acquisition and our conception of meaning in language, and even that we must show how the former is embedded within the latter.

(c) The theory must be valid for contexts of language use in which there is no ambiguity, where understanding, so to speak, 'goes without saying'. The theory must also hold for contexts in which one is, on the contrary, led to *seek* the meaning of what is said (contexts of meaning-resistance).

The question view of language, which I have called the *problematological conception of language* (cf. Meyer 1981, 1982), enables us, I think, to meet these requirements. To be fair to Gadamer, I ought to add that he uses Collingwood's theory of questioning to study the phenomenon of interpretation. But he fails to systematize it. He does not extend it to an overall conception of language, as if one could develop a theory of language without a theory of interpretation and, conversely, as if the intrinsic nature of language and of the dynamic of questioning (and answering) were heterogeneous to some degree. Questioning is a process of interaction between an interpreter and what is to be interpreted (the *interpretandum*); the interpretandum bears no trace of any interrogative structure of markers that could, and should, justify a conception of understanding made in terms of questioning. In fact, hermeneuticists do not even know how questioning works. As a consequence, some of them came to dis-agree with Gadamer as to the origin of the questions raised by texts: is the source of these questions to be found in the text or, as Jauss contends, in the reader? But this is another story, one to which we will return later.

Gadamer's view is that questioning as a mechanism is distinct from textuali-ty, which cannot be the case. The apocritico-problematological structure of language and the interrogative nature of rhetoric characterize textuality and make understanding a questioning process. The phenomenon of language as much as that of understanding needs to be referred back to questioning as a common root.

6.2. Answerhood as meaning

Meaning is a question-answer relationship. Knowing the meaning of a dis-course is identical to knowing the status of the discourse in question as an answer. But which question do we allude to when we use the term 'the discourse in question' and which question is the discourse then seen as answering?

Meaning is an intrinsic feature of language. Whatever we say or write must deal with a question, which implies that our discourse must be meaningful. When we use language, we *mean* something. All discourse *has* meaning though it does not necessarily *give* meaning. Discourse would do this, however, if, *quod non*, it were always saying *that* it means *what* it means. But the object of discourse, in general, is not to say that it means what it means, but to say it without further ado. In problematological terms, this means that we encounter answers which do not directly say what question they answer or in what sense they are propounded as answers. Answers thus repress their status as answers. They are answers and hence they have meaning; they do not say that they are answers and state that they mean this or that. But they could state it if the question (of meaning) was raised. The question of the status of some statement or text as an answer is not the same as the question in response to which the statement or text was originally made. However, statements and texts give an indirect answer to the question they respond to since they *are* meaningful.

Thus the question of meaning does not correspond to the question that it directly answers; statements and texts do not answer questions about their status as answers. If we want to know what some text means, we must *ask* for its meaning. Our answer will then stipulate which question is raised in the answer under consideration.

When we investigate a text to determine its meaning, two situations are possible: we may know the meaning of a text because it is obvious what it is an answer to; or we do not know its meaning and are forced to ask the question. In the first case, what is in question can be immediately derived from the text itself. In the second case, we must investigate the text to find out what it means. In both cases, the interpreter asks himself what the text means; however, he does it differently in each case. Answers make themselves autonomous with respect to the questions that gave rise to them and thus become problematological expressions. Therefore, any answer is in itself a question. In other words, when faced with a sentence or a text, we are questioned and consequently must answer: we agree or disagree, we comment or add, we tacitly accept the answer or tacitly reject it, or we answer to its presence by simply not being interested in its being an answer because, for instance, we are not interested in the question it addresses.

A text raises the question it deals with in the mind of its readers. This is not due to some intrinsic indetermination of texts (Iser) but to the apocritico-problematological nature of discourse in general. The readers are led to question the text as to its suitability as an answer to this question. A rejection or acceptance of the answer is only possible if the text's adequacy as an answer to the question it *means* to solve is questioned.

To put our arguments in a nutshell, the status of statements and texts as answers is in and by itself a question. In more technical terms, we can say that all answers are problematological and apocritical.

A dialectical dimension is then inherent in textuality: texts request a response from those who read or hear them. They contain an implied reader, i.e. a potential questioner.

The dialectical reality of textuality does not imply the existence of an actual dialogue between the text and the reader. After all, only people, not texts, answer questions. This reservation is not without consequences. As discussed earlier, the extent to which the question view is valid can only be defined dialectically. A substitutional answer can only be offered in response to the question of meaning when, as in the case of dialogues, propositions can be singled out and when a non-literal reading of the proposition in question is not considered. The reasons for this are obvious. In a dialogue, both interlocutors are supposed to discuss the same question. Even if one of them merely wants to respond in a different way, he must first know what is in question and must take this question over in his speech, so to speak. Both interlocutors must perceive the same meaning in the question they discuss. If a question about the meaning of some particular proposition is actually raised, an answer to this question can then be made by explicitly substituting an equivalent statement for the one in question.

The substitution view of meaning is then confined to specific dialogical situations. But if this theory seems to hold at all in such situations, this is not because it is valid, but rather because meaning can be explained by substituting a different statement for the one in question. Such meaning by substitution can only be justified in terms of the conditioned questioning peculiar to dialogues. Meaning as substitution is actually a special case of a more general process in which one relates an answer to a question via another answer which, in the case here, answers *the same* question literally.

As a theory of meaning, the substitution view thus fails in terms of its own principles. Obviously, substitution is possible only because one question is literally and unambiguously under discussion. The substitution view, however, bases its claim to validity on the substitution of autonomous sentences, which are to be considered independently of the question(s) they are meant to answer. When the substitution view is right, it is for the wrong reasons. As a *theory* of language, it must be discarded.

When the meaning of a single statement is in question, meaning can be expressed by substituting one proposition for another. But even in this case, meaning is an answer. The substitutional statement is in fact a problematological answer since it expresses the speaker's question as an answer to the addressee's hermeneutic inquiry.

This reveals what happens during the interpretative process: understanding substitutes one answer for another, the first answer expressing the question corresponding to the second answer. Meaning, however, is not understanding: it is the link between the problematological answer and the apocritical one. Understanding leads from one answer to another answer. It may be seen as a substitution, or at any rate, as a process of substitution. The result, however, which is what we call meaning, is not the logical equivalence of one statement to another. Meaning and that which is meant are problematologically equivalent in the sense that they both relate to the same question, but generally they are not apocritically substitutable for one another; literally, they say different things, although, according to the circumstances, they can be related to the degree of being figuratively equivalent. *Figurative equivalence* does not mean *adequate translation*, nor does it imply that we have a substitute for the text being interpreted. Rather, figurative equivalence means that we know *a* problematic that gives a consistent answer to our question concerning the question(s) raised by the text.

6.3. *The hermeneutic question and its answer*

Our starting point is a given answer: it does not matter whether it is a statement or a text. What we seek is an adequate description of what happens when we understand this answer.

The author of this answer is a questioner. When he produced it, he had a question in mind and he responded to that question with an answer. This answer is presented, say, as a statement. The question that this statement raises is that of its status as an answer, since this statement forces the reader to ask what qualifies it as an answer and what question it actually solves. Since the answer is not presented with explicit reference to a specific question, it is basic to the autonomy of the statement that the reader be asked. Most of the time, the reader does not notice that he is asked anything; instead, he responds to the question automatically. This fact reveals the autonomy of answers as statements with respect to the questions which they were originally conceived of as responses to. Language, however, is meant to answer or express questions. An autonomous answer is not defined in reference to *a* particular question, for it can answer other questions *or* express them, provided that the problematological difference between the expressed and the answered question is respected. Even if an answer is autonomous with respect to a given *and known* question, it can nonetheless raise and express other questions as well. In the understanding process, the interpreter establishes, rediscovers, or simply gets acquainted with this relationship between a question and its answer.

The answer is apocritical with respect to the question raised. It implies the repression (*Verdrängung*) of its answerhood: the answer in the form of a statement says *something*, and attention is paid chiefly to this *something*. Someone other than the speaker or the author of the answer is confronted with the answer. This answer is perceived as an answer and the question of its status as an answer is thereby raised. The addressee can, in turn, come up with the question which characterizes the answer as such. If it not directly understandable, the answer becomes *a real question for this addressee* that must be expressly addressed. The question that is problematological then becomes problematic as well. The question dealt with cannot be directly read from the answer and the answerhood of the answer becomes a question to be answered. The interpretative process is a questioning that will have an answer; as such, the answer will be apocritical with respect to the speaker's question, the latter being problematological in the eyes of the exegete. If the speaker had expressed his problem with a statement before answering it, this statement would have had a problematological answer while the solution of the speaker's problem would have been apocritical. The interpreter proceeds inversely: he considers the speaker's answer as problematological and the answer giving the speaker's question is apocritical with respect to the interpreter's query. The problematological difference is then respected in the case of each question. Let us emphasize again that the interpreter's question, which bears on the explicitation of the original question accounting for the meaningfulness of some answer is *not* the same the question the speaker originally responded to and meant to answer with what he said. Both questioning processes, the original and the hermeneutic, must be distinguished.

We would also note that this movement of inference or understanding is the inverse of the process of producing an answer; it is as if, in some sense, the addressee was putting himself in the place of the author in order to interpret, i.e. discover, what he meant. The starting point of the interpretative inference, however, is not the author's mind or life but his text.

The relationship between meaning and what is meant is one of equivalence. Interpretation is clearly a process of substituting answers. Interpretation seeks to make explicit the question from which the answer in question originates. The production of the answer is the inverse of the hermeneutic questioning process with the difference that the original question had never been explicitly asked. Interpretation must be substitutional in the sense that what is apocritical for the speaker is problematological for the addressee and vice versa.

Interpretation is substitution for reasons totally different from those given by the substitution view. No privilege is granted to propositions and consequently to logical equivalence. Interrogative expansion is after all only one way among others to relate an answer to the question it deals with. Literal readings are the essence of this kind of substitution. Even a literally substitutional reading of an answer rests upon the question view of meaning. Substitution characterizes understanding and meaning since the act of relating an answer to its answerhood is tantamount to *passing* from an answer to another, one that specifies *what* is answered in the first one. The assertoric content of that which is meant is left unaltered in the meaning, which renders explicit *what* the original answer says. This is necessary since the original answer merely states *what* it states without affirming *that* it states it.

The fact that the process of interpretation substitutes one answer for the answer that is interpreted does not imply that meaning – i.e. the result of the interpretation process – is a literal translation of the first answer. Understanding renders explicit the question the original answer solves and can do so figurative-ly. Besides, nothing implies that we substitute only *one* answer for each single statement, especially in the case of longer texts. Meaning is not necessarily a paraphrase. Indeed, paraphrasing even becomes impossible when we are faced with texts. Literal equivalence or paraphrase is possible only when we can directly read in the answer the question dealt with, which, in turn, is possible only if the structure of the sentence is sufficient to perform this reading without any help from context. But texts present themselves as wholes.

This decription of meaning, however, may be misleading. It could suggest that meaning is referentially substitutional. The substitution of one answer for another in the interpretation process does not result in a formulation of the original statement's meaning that is merely a paraphrase of it. Meaning merely stipulates the question the original statement addressed. On the other hand, meaning *can* be a literal reformulation of a statement. When the question dealt with in the answer can be read in the answer itself, the meaning will be a para-phrase as example (2) is with respect to (1). The structure of the statement enables the interpreter to develop a literal reading or a paraphrase of the state-ment.

The sole requirement that constitutes the definition of meaning does not imply that the hermeneutic answer must be logically equivalent, or that it must be a single statement for *each* answer considered. Obviously, both these con-ditions do not hold for texts. Texts present themselves as wholes. What is said is always problematized, but is the case of texts, it is not *one* answer which is in question. A whole set of interrelated questions are raised which form a *problematic*. This problematic or text must be understood as a whole, i.e. as what it is. *What* a text says is not directly derivable from one single state-ment, nor does it result in one statement, let alone a paraphrase. That is where textuality, i.e. *poiesis*, obviously has a hermeneutic bearing. The question(s) a text *as a whole* raise(s) is (or are) determined by the very structure of the whole, i.e. by textuality. A text is an answer and raises the question of what it answers. The sentences of the text as considered in a non-literal reading ask this question. The textuality of a text is the question implied *by* the sentences of the text although this question is not answered *in* these individual sentences.

To use quite general terms, the relationship between meaning and that which is meant is one of problematological equivalence. In order to verify this, we should inquire into their relationship *as answers*. The given answer is problem-atological as much as the hermeneutic answer: they are problematologically equivalent, though not necessarily apocritically equivalent. This problematological equivalence mirrors the substitutive movement of understanding and the possible absence of literal equivalence that arises from the process of interpretation. Meaning is problematologically a substitution. A good example of this is example (9) considered earlier. Answers raise questions. This fact itself raises more questions.

(a) An answer suggests not only the question of its own answerhood but also many other questions. They are unspecified by what is literally said.

(b) What is the origin of the questions implied *by* literary texts?

The second question requires an extensive treatment since conflicting opinions may be held about it. As to the first question, it is clear that many questions can be associated with a single answer. One can even know the question a statement answers and still ask other questions about the answers in relation to other questions and answers. The reason is that answers make themselves autonomous with respect to the questions from which they originate. They are problematological. Among the questions raised, we find the question of their meaning, i.e. of the question to which they answer. If this question is present in the literal structure of the answer, we (as interpreters) can directly perceive it and determine what the answer means. Explicitly, this would give rise to an interrogative expansion. Since we are ourselves language users, we are questioners. When faced with some piece of language, we answer on the basis of what is said, if only implicitly, and relate what is said to its status as an answer.

6.4. *Textuality as the meeting point of poetics and hermeneutics*

The relationship between a text as a whole and its constituent sentences is defined as a question-answer complex. As such, it brings the problematological difference into play poetically, that is, quite specifically. Form is meant to express this difference.

Furthermore, the relationship between textuality and the sentences in a text is, from an hermeneutical point of view, the same as the one prevailing between figurative meaning and literal reading, what is implicit and what is explicit. Such a relationship is also a question-answer complex. We can easily verify this by returning to one of our previous examples, to which we intentionally ascribed a non-literal reading. (9) *It is one o'clock* can mean several things like 'Let's have lunch' or 'Let's go', or even 'We still have time to keep on talking'. To each of these readings is associated one question to which (9) answers in the last analysis. *It is one o'clock* does not answer the question *What time is it?*, though it does literally, but the question *What do we do now?*, for instance. This latter question is figuratively implied by (9). Such an implication can follow in either of two ways, provided that the problematological difference is always respected. An answer *either* answers something other than the direct question it answers, *or* it raises another question that it actually answers. In the first case, the answer is considered as apocritical but implicitly refers back to another question which explains what the answer fundamentally means and why it was propounded. In the second case, the answer is considered problematological: it expresses a question, or an enigma — like a metaphor — that we, the readers, are asked to answer. It literally asks for a non-literal reading that will be the final answer. The answerhood of the first answer is then known, and hence its meaning. In the first case, the answer is propounded as an answer, but to a different question, which is implicitly suggested, whereas, in the second case, that which is implicitly implied by the answer is another answer.

In both cases, a question is implicitly or explicitly asked that differs from the one that is solved and directly treated in the answer itself. What is explicit differs from what is implicit, as a question differs from an answer (problematological difference).

We could say that a text is figurative with respect to its literal meaning. We could also affirm that textuality is the literal expression of something that is textually figurative. In fact, both formulations cover the same reality. The text asks for its own reading without literally raising the question. The answer is then figurative with respect to what the text literally affirms in its constituent sentences. On the other hand, the text is figurative of a literal reading. i.e. it is the figurative embodiment of a non-literary truth. When we examine carefully the difference between the figurative and the literal, it clearly appears that we are not faced with a difference in nature but in function.

(a) Such a difference is an hermeneutic one. It belongs to some meta-level of discourse, that of interpretation. It is *used*, in hermeneutics, to indicate that we are confronted with a duality of meaning.

(b) Such a duality is necessarily of an argumentative or a rhetorical nature. The relationship between the two readings involved is that between two answers for two questions, which are themselves related by some question-answer complex that characterizes the inference to be made. It is then a manifestation or a consequence of the problematological difference.

(c) A literal reading of a sentence or set of sentences can be intrinsically defined in terms of interrogative clauses.

The interpretation of a literary text is a non-literary text. It is not a reformulation duplicating the original text. The interpretative or hermeneutic answer only stipulates which questions the text in question answers. This answer is implied *by* the text in a non-literal way, but is itself non-literary, i.e. non-figurative, since it is itself an answer to the hermeneutic question. The difference between the figurative and literal reading must then be qualified more fully. The question dealt with *by* the text is provided literally as the non-literal question implied by the text. This question is formulated *via* a problematological answer that literally expresses it. This answer is itself the non-literal substitute for the text: it is problematologically equivalent with it but not identical to it as far as its apocritical and assertoric content is concerned. *It is one o'clock* is not literally, i.e. apocritically, equivalent with *Let's have lunch now*, since , as answers, they do not answer the same question, and if they do, it is only an accident of context. We cannot reasonably say that they literally mean the same thing. In the case under consideration, however, they mean the same thing because one says (9) in order to ask someone to infer that it is time to go to lunch. The question indirectly raised *by* (9) is answered by the assertion *Let's have lunch now*. As answers, they are equivalent only to the extent that they both relate to a deeper and indirect problem of what to do together at a certain time.

The meaning of a text which expresses its meaning non-literally, i.e. indirectly is then figurative with respect to what that text says literally. As a text, however, it *is* something else, namely a non-literal answer. Textual meaning is non-literal with regard to the various literal readings contained *in* the text, but it is the literal formulation of that figurative answer.

Consequently, we can view a text as a figurative answer raised by the textuality of the constituent sentences of the text, or as the literal expression of what is figuratively suggested in the text considered as a whole. With the first view, we privilege answers *qua* answers while, in the second case, the same results are attained by privileging the questions involved.

What is essential to note in all this is that we cannot replace a literal reading by a figural expression as if they were literally equivalent, i.e. apocritically equivalent with respect to some identical question.

In both cases, there is a varying proportion of literal to non-literal expressions. Literariness and textuality are related according to the basic law of the textual auto-contextualization of the problematological difference. The less explicit the problematic in the text, the more the form must suggest it and make sense of it. The whole text must then be submitted to a second-level reading. The distinction between figurative and literal meaning vanishes since, in the case under consideration, the problem is textually suggested and is not literally expressed in the sentences themselves. The latter affirm something else which, in order to be understood, must be related to the whole textuality.

In the reverse case, we are confronted with a problem that is literally stipulated, as in detective stories, for instance. What is figuratively present in this unfolding is the textual embedding of sentences into a sequential and temporal order. The resolution of the plot takes time, which the temporality of reading follows. The text as a whole does not need a second-level reading to receive an interpretation. The problem put forth at the beginning is solved at the end, and apart from the strictly ideological background and framework of the story, there is nothing more to it to understand. The text as a whole has *no other* figural reading than the exigency to read the story as it materially and physically presents itself. Nothing else is asked at the level of the text, as if the literal readings of the sentences were self-sufficient.

Hermetic or problematic poetry, on the other hand, has no reading which could be made without appeal to the text *as a whole*. Textuality, here, requires a retroactive process from the reader. The purpose of this process is to enable the reader to grasp the text as a whole, and to go beyond the additive reading of each individual sentence or verse. The problem is not literally expressed; it must be figuratively suggested, and it is up to the text to make this suggestion. It is not *in* the text that the solution lies but rather in the text *qua* text, i.e. in the arrangement and embedding of a problem. Such an embedding is never literally stated. The relationship between the questions raised by a text and the content of the text remains unspecified in the text itself. Even if the problem were rendered explicit, the solution would not express such a relationship but merely the problem.

The role of textuality varies as a function of the process of auto-contextualizing problems. The more a text is stylistically built up, the more is textuality the key to understanding, whereas, in the opposite case, the role of textuality is restricted to that of a temporal ordering. Meaning, then, unveils itself temporally rather than structurally: the problem and its solution become known as a result of a mere progressive reading.

6.5. *Where do we find the questions answered by a text?*

When we look for the meaning of a text, we try to find the questions to which it answers as a text. This is, as said earlier, the basic tenet of the problematological conception of meaning.

(a) Rhetoricalization deals in a specific way with questions and thereby generates fiction as answers. *Poietics*, as we know, is the way in which textuality materializes itself literarily, i.e. auto-contextualizes the problems that it represents. *Rhetoric*, here, is the discursive process that takes place to bring about auto-contextualization.

Rhetoric operates on two levels. Fiction asks its questions rhetorically with respect to the ideas transmitted by some thought system. Fiction *is* the rhetoricalization of non-rhetorical questions that the system must face. It performs such a task by creating a discourse for which those ideas serve as answers without having ever been questioned. In that sense, fiction is argumentative: it answers ideological questions indirectly through non-ideological questions. Textual answers are, here, rhetorical *stricto sensu*: they refer back to questions that are not actually raised as questions. Their solution is held *a priori*. The rhetoricalization of the original ideological problems is called fiction. This process defines the fictionality of the answering text.

The question dealt with through the text and figuratively asked *in* the text by the textuality – i.e. the ordering of interrelated sentences of the text – has an answer that some critics deem to be in the text and some others outside of it. Rhetoricalization fulfills its other function at this level. Auto-contextualization treats a problem by rhetorically stipulating its solution. The problem is asked all the more when it is figuratively represented in the literal content of the text. The problem is specified all the more literally when its textual solution can be explicitly demarcated within the text. In the latter case the rhetoric of textuality is closer to everyday language than in the former. The solution literally expresses the problem as that which is solved *in* the text, that is, here, *by* the text.

Nevertheless, the problem which consists in relating a given problem literally present in the text to its textual solution is not *said* in the text. It is a problem implied *by* the text to some extent. The problem(s) to which a given text directly answers, although non-ideological, remain(s) more or less non-literal with regard to the various sentences composing the text. Rhetoric, here, is the way we can know this problem, and hence the meaning of the text, from what is said in the text.

(b) Since they are literally unexpressed in a text, the question(s) that the text answers are open to discussion and to interpretation. This absence from the text has given rise to various *hermeneutic commitments*. What lies outside the text and still influences it? The author and his or her psychology and social environment in one possible answer. We have seen why such a hypothesis should not be retained in spite of its partial truth. This view is partially true on account of the existence of an ideological background underlying every literary work, however transformed it may appear as a fiction with respect to societal problems posed by a given thought system. On the other hand, the author masks himself in the fiction he writes, even though in some manner it expresses his deepest nature. What he writes acquires as much autonomy with respect to some particular ideological background as it does with respect to his 'unconscious'. This autonomy creates a gap or a veil which renders it impossible to equate the textuality of the text analyzed with the subjective feelings of its author. The link that remains can shed light on the text, but what it means and how it is poetically structured cannot be reduced to that link. Sartre's *Nausea* may be related to the author's ugliness and the reactions it occasioned in others. It can also be viewed as the expression of a social view of bourgeois values and society. But it means something else. Among other things, it is a description of the questionableness of the world when our existence appears more and more absurd and meaningless to us. This explains why *Nausea* can please good-looking people and the uncommitted from a political point of view. The true meaning of Sartre's book is lost when it is related only to the psychology of its author: strikingly enough, we usually hear such an association made when our interlocutor wants to discredit the book instead of understand it. In sum, when works trouble us for some reason or other, psychological arguments come to the fore.

There is a widespread line of reasoning concerned with textual meaning. One does not speak of *intentions* or *unconscious motives*, which are non-textual concepts, but one speaks of a second text as the key to the one to be explained. The relationship between the two texts is *structural*. Authors' intentions or personality have nothing to do with these structural homologies. Language and texts speak through them, even in spite of them; a textual unconscious substitutes for a personal unconscious.

Structuralism has often been associated with some kind of elitism. Who knows what the keys of interpretation are? Not the author himself, who cannot mean what he said. It is the literary critic who, by comparing myths or tales, for instance, spots structural homologies. Texts can then be analyzed and dissected in function of structural relations which can be grasped only on the basis of a cumulative knowledge of various tales, myths, and narratives. One text, let alone one author, does not mean anything by itself. "I thus do not aim to show how men think in myths but how myths think in men, unbeknownst to them" (Levi-Strauss 1972: 20; cited in Culler 1975: 50). Comparisons are necessary and require an abundant quantity of similar materials to take place at all. Culler, maybe more than anybody alse, has underlined with particular accuracy the difficulties posed by the structuralist view of meaning.

"Levi-Strauss claims that meaning is revealed by comparing myths, but the differences between the two myths drawn from different cultures are not used to communicate anything." (Culler 1975: 49)

A text functions as a sign for something else but does not mean anything by itself. The opposition of the raw and the cooked, for instance, should not be read as if these concepts, instead of others, had significance. They mean the opposition of nature and culture and any other symbolic complex would do as well. The literal content of narratives or myths does not even function as a problem as to what they mean as such, i.e. as to what they refer to *by virtue* of their literal readings. Terms do not count, nor does what they refer to: they only form a pretext that suggests something else in opposition to other terms. Who will choose the binary oppositions into which texts will be cut? By comparison with other texts, perhaps, we may find similarities, but this begs the question of knowing how we find such structural homologies in the first place if we do not know them beforehand or if, somehow, we do not have a reading grid. There is even some circularity involved in the structuralist theory of textuality. A myth, for instance, is unintelligible if one does not resort to other myths. The content does not count, only the structure does. The problem remains of knowing how to choose isomorphic myths. Do we not beg the question in proceeding to such a choice? This procedure may well work on various occasions, for reasons which structuralists themselves would deny, but we would surely not accept it as a general theory of meaning.

"Two items can be compared on a variety of grounds; which grounds will yield pertinent relations?" (Culler 1975: 46)

Relevance must be taken into account, which means that we will have problems whose solutions are related by exclusion or inclusion. After all,

"There is no *a priori* reason to think that the myths have anything to do with one another." (Culler 1975: 47)

If they do, the question of their relatonship is begged but not answered after such a comparison has been made. Besides, structural analogies can always be found between two texts: which analogies will be the ones that count? Another problem is how extended or complete a corpus of texts should be in order for us to get at the meaning of one of them?

> "Here, as in *Système de la mode* (Barthes), one can observe the insufficiencies of a particular interpretation of structural linguistics: the notion that in studying a corpus one can discover the grammar or logic of a system through the division and comparison of forms may lead to a neglect of the basic problem of determining precisely what is to be explained." (Culler 1975: 49)

Do all these criticisms leveled against structuralism imply that we are here facing a completely erroneous theory of textuality? If not, the question of knowing what is valid in structuralism inevitably arises. There are partial truths in the structuralist theory, but they are treated paradoxically. The paradox of structuralism is based on two correct propositions which are inadequately integrated from a theoretical point of view, though they can lead to interesting punctual analyses in a application. On the one hand, it is true that any text has an objective meaning, independently of its author's intention. The textuality of the text that renders it objective is not to be found in this text itself, however. On the other hand, we are also ready to say that the meaning of a text is not a literal reformulation of its referential counterpart. The signified of the text as a signifier is another signifier and not a thing nor a piece of reality. But where should we stop in our progression from text to text? Has literal meaning no role to play at all?

Structuralism, as we know, arose as a reaction against the old view that the meaning of a text rests upon the psychology of its author, that is, broadly speaking, on authorship. The key of a text is a text, another text in which the essential features of the original one are transferred. In the second text, however, these features are represented otherwise. The structuralist answer is that features are displaced as binary oppositions (why?) into other binary oppositions.

Our contention concerning such a displacement is that we cannot grant it any validity without resorting to the question view. Binary oppositions are the two sides of answerhood. Alternatives refer back to some question and represent its *yes* or *no*. Textual displacement, as the structuralists see it, is nothing but the fictionalization of a question through another one. The questions which are fictionalized are mythologized in societies where literature and fiction overlap, and serve as the foundation of ideology. My objection to the structuralist view is that it neglects questioning, only to consider some derived manifestations such as possible 'answers', i.e. alternatives.

The fact that structuralism has emerged as a reaction against the tendency to look for the meaning of texts outside textuality is no accident of history. The very possibility of an hermeneutic opposition between, say, structuralism and the theories based on intentionality has its roots in the basic structure of hermeneutic questioning. This opposition is but a particular case of something inherent in questioning when applied to texts. To characterize the alternative briefly, we shall say that structuralism, on the one hand, sees meaning as textual and that psychologism, on the other hand, views it as extra-textual.

Such an alternative amounts to the following dilemma: any given text answers its author's questions as much as those of the readers. The opposition between structuralism and reception theory, for instance, is then an example of this dilemma. The latter finds its justification in the fact that the question of answerhood is neither explicitly, nor thematically answered in the text, which affirms something other than its meaning while meaning it. Meaning seems to be evanescent and to lie outside the text. Where, then, if not in some implied author or implied reader? On the other hand, the meaning of a text is another text, and not an intention or a psychoanalytical description, much less a social picture of the times. Meaning is textual and is not to be found *in* the original text. It is itself some piece of language: it is another text. Texts are texts of other texts: in some sense, a text is an answer to another text. Textual autonomy with respect to the questions which initiated this textual answering arises from the fictionalization of available texts or textual information already known. *Textual autonomy* is nothing but *textual dependence*, but *vis-à-vis* other texts to which they somehow answer or which are somehow their answers.

Textual autonomy with respect to questions rooted in a particular epoch relates texts to one another through the various ideas they represent or repress. The history of ideas or the history of problems – which is still an undeveloped discipline or approach among scholars – is possible by virtue of an intellectual filiation crossing over socio-historical determinations. The latter do count in the genesis of textual answers, but those answers acquire an autonomy which enables scholars to see in their succession a development of ideas, for which the key word is *influence*. Texts reply to one another, as if their origin in particular times were secondary.

The fact that such an outlook is possible does not mean that it is right. We now see why it is possible. It is nonetheless a limiting approach, for which one should at last substitute a history of problems that does not deny the autonomy of ideas but simply indicates what it is that they are autonomous in respect to. The closer to everyday life a text is, the less autonomous and the less meaningful it is in terms of other texts in the tradition. A text that is very far from everyday life becomes naturally autonomous and clearly requires some appeal to so-called textual influences to appear fully meaningful.

Structuralism is an attempt to capture the textuality of texts, i.e. the way in which texts are displaced into other ones which apparently deal with other problems. Basically, then, structuralism is right in regarding meaning through the optic of binary opposites, which each refer to some definite question. It nonetheless fails to realize that binary oppositions are the apocritical counterpart of questions. Questions are absent from the structuralist framework, and this is our main reservation. It is hard to accept the idea that the meaning of some particular text is not even dependent upon the intrinsic content of the text. As to the unfolding of the problematic, it seems fairly obvious that some story or tale, for instance, evolves from a situation A / not A to a new one B / not B, and so on. In other words, there is a problematological substitution, constituted by the narrative process itself, of the problem A? B? to C? We must understand problems, i.e. the terms of binary oppositions, in terms of other problems expressing them as equivalent in some respect.

The dilemma mentioned earlier is an intrinsic feature of textuality. Even when textuality is conceived in terms of questioning, theorists fail to realize this 'structural' dialectics of questioning. The debate between Jauss and Gadamer illustrates this quite clearly.

According to Gadamer (1975a: 333), the transcendence of meaning must be attributed to the unstipulated question to which a text answers.

"We can understand a text, only when we have understood the question to which it is an answer."

Do we then understand this question when we understand what it is a reply to, and so forth?

The adequacy of the author's intention and meaning to its aesthetic reply enables the interpreter to conclude that the author exactly and precisely meant what he wrote (Cf. Gadamer 1975a: 333).

This Collingwoodian approach is contested by the upholders of the so-called *Rezeptionsästhetik*, represented by the writings of Jauss.

The main thrust of Jauss's criticism of Gadamer runs as follows. There is no immutable and unique meaning attached to any given text. The plurality of consistent readings is a fact. Their variation according to changing ideological contexts is another fact. The very idea that tradition is conceived as the key to meaning is itself a social way of 'receiving' texts. It corresponds, in fact, to the need felt by some German intellectuals, mostly conservative, to cling to a glorious past which was destroyed by the world wars, that is, to cling to the 'world that we lost'.

According to Jauss (1978: 61), there is no such thing as a question embodied in the text itself, independently of another questioner who would raise it. Questions do not persist in the Platonic world of tradition. The text itself, according to Gadamer, has 'its' meaning once and for all. Present time only actualizes what is eternal. This obviously leads to the hypostatization of the question and to its meaningfulness in itself. The texts even seem to lie outside of time. The interpreter merely reproduces the text in his interpretation. How can we sustain the idea that there would be *one* meaning, the true one?

All this, Jauss stresses, does not prevent Gadamer from speaking of the fusion of past and present, the original questioner, i.e. the author, and the contemporary questioner, i.e. the interpreter, as if the latter had a constitutive role to play in this *Horizontverschmelzung*, in order to bring meaning to light. Jauss sees in the intervention of the reader-interpreter a contradiction with Gadamer's reification of the Tradition which speaks for itself to us, like the Heideggerian Being.

> "Même les grandes oeuvres littéraires du passé ne sont pas reçues et comprises par le fait d'un pouvoir de médiation qui leur serait inhérent, et l'effet qu'elles produisent ne peut être comparé avec une émanation". (Jauss 1978: 62)

As Wiesenthal (1979: 63) puts it:

> "The difference between the two conceptions becomes clear when one asks the question of knowing how to decide that we face an aesthetic judgment. According to Jauss, it is determined by the reader, whereas for Kaiser, it is a characteristic of the text itself." (translation mine)

Kaiser and Gadamer uphold the same view on this.

According to *Rezeptionsästhetik*, there is no immanence of the questions in the texts, even if it is recognized that the knowledge of the question can be equated with meaning. The questions to be asked rest upon the reader's understanding of the problematic. The text may offer different answers and permit different interpretations, which evolve with historical change. This variation is essentially due to changes in the questions asked. After all, a Marxist and a scholastic philosopher do not ask the same questions about Plato's doctrines. The outlook changes and manifests itself through the questions raised. This is how, for example, Jauss analyzes Goethe's and Racine's *Iphigenie*. The topic is apparently identical, as the title of the play let us think, but Goethe's play addressed a different question than Racine's (cf. Jauss 1978: 226ff.).

Both theories are right to some extent, and could be expected to be so on the basis of the problematological conception. But they also run into undeniable difficulties that the problematological conception can help us avoid.

Gadamer is wrong when he claims that the questions that give access to textual meaning must be found either in the text and / or in the author. They are not *in* the text but implied *by* it, as figurative meaning asks for literal reading. But they are not 'in the author' either because they could not literally be found within the text itself. There is no necessary or intrinsic adequation between an author's questions and the textual answer that arises from them. A text means something by itself too, independently of the author's intentions, though this does not imply that such a meaning is *in* the text.

Interpretations change. Jauss must nonetheless face other theoretical difficulties. If the meaning of any given text depends solely upon the readers' questions, we may perhaps have explained why the same text can be interpreted differently through time, but we have no textual and objective criterion for judging the validity of these interpretations. The fact that they emerged seems sufficient to explain that they had to emerge, at least from a social, historical, or political point of view. All the interpretations undergone by some text may be understood in terms of their contexts without being allowed by the text itself.

The opposition between Gadamer and Jauss can therefore be summed up as the dilemma between interpretative immobilism (or conservatism) and hermeneutic relativism (which is supposedly progressive).

6.6. *Textual dialectics*

Literary texts are figurative. What they literally express refers to a non-literal question, though the answer expressing this question ought to be understood literally. The opposition between the literal and the figurative should not be taken literally, but as the textual embodiment of the problematological difference.

A text is an answer. It deals with various questions through what it affirms. The unity of the written is called the text. The textuality of the text is non-literal with respect to each of the propositions contained within it. It is the question raised by the arrangement of these literal readings; as an answer, it is the literal answer with respect to the figurative content.

The plurality of answers is rooted in textual figurativeness, that is, in the problematological aspect of literature. Possible answers are simultaneously compatible with one another on the level of the text and require a reader to actualize them as answers. These readings are textually embedded and can change with new historical determinations which *make* reading a *pragmatic* procedure. There is always a pragmatic dimension in reading. Structuralism sees texts as closed entities. But they are not so. The hermeneutic circle, which closes a text upon itself at the level of understanding, is highly questionable. When there is only a first-level reading due to the necessity of one reading only, *viz.* the temporally progressive, no retroactive grasp is required from the reader. As for those texts that require a second-level or retroactive reading, the circle between the beginning and the end has nothing to do with a hermeneutic circle in the sense of Heidegger, for instance. There is no totality to break by stepping in. Access is not conditioned by some *Sprung* but by a referential reading accompanied by a background movement, i.e. a process of re-totalizing textuality as such.

In addition, we must realize that the questions literary texts answer — since we now know that such questions are plural — cannot be furnished by the author but must be derivable from the texts themselves. More than any other texts, literary texts are subject to plural readings, i.e. to the duality of the figurative and the literal. As seen previously, such a duality is a materialization of the problematological difference and should not be taken at its face value: it is a functional dichotomy.

The problematological conception of reading and understanding is clearly rooted in the correlative theory of language. Any text raises a question. What is in question is suggested as a question through the answer which treats it as solved. If John, for instance, wants to be elected to some office and I make a speech saying *John is honest*, my affirmation suggests that John *could* be dishonest, though I explicitly deny it. Such a question is in fact implied by my denial itself. The question comes to the fore by being answered. It thereby comes to the attention of my interlocutor as a question. He can then propose a different answer, that is, think about the question differently. In the above example, my affirmation is meant to cast a doubt on John's honesty in an oblique way. This can only be achieved if there is a question raised by what is said. Whatever the addressee's subsequent reaction to the question, i.e. to the answer, the meaning is known when the answer and the question to which it is an answer are associated in the mind of the addressee. The question raised by the author's answer is inscribed within the textual structure of this answer. The literal reading of the latter, in the case of texts, makes such a decoding possible. The reader's answer provides the author's question, which can be inquired independently but complementarily (Schleiermacher) through an analysis of the text itself. The author is an implied author: it is the intentional unity which can be construed on the basis of the text (which objectively has a finite range of implied readings) in accordance to real-life elements concerning the author and his time.

The reader's problem is to have a (problematological) answer accounting for the text as an apocritical answer. An analysis of intentionality *may* help the textual research by shedding light on the link between text and problems. However, the question raised by the text must be questioned by some reader: even if the text 'gives' some answer, the nature of the latter, though rooted in the text or implied by it, is dependent upon the question asked. For us, the implied author 'Plato' has said things that his contemporaries were not interested in, for instance. This fact does not signify that *we*, or *they*, put in Plato's mind assertions which cannot be corroborated by his text. It simply means that we are not questioning the text in the same way, that the answers once given are not answers to *our* problems. But they are nonetheless answers, as much as ours. They are interpretations among others which are compatible with what is literally said in Plato's texts. They are possible ways to qualify what is in question in his writings, possible in the sense that they are compatible with the literal readings to be found in the text.

The relationship between the questions implied by a text, giving rise to its various interpretations, and the questions literally answered in the text on which objective textual analysis is based is that of a gap. It is left to historical context, broadly speaking, to bridge that gap: the questions asked by the reader will give a content to the implied textuality of the text, to the implied questions raised *by* a text *in* its literal, i.e. objective, content. History, and history alone, renders implicit questions explicit and makes a text the figurative expression of a contemporary interest. The plurality of interpretations is embedded in the text itself, as much as any explicit question concerning a given text is implicitly, i.e. non-literally, asked by the text as a text. We only find an implied implicitness of a text when we are prepared to *raise* these questions.

The questions addressed as to the meaning of a given text bear upon the text's status as an answer. This fact implies that there is a textual counterpart to our answers which renders the latter 'objective', i.e. limited by the literal readings allowed by the text. This is a strong argumentation in favor of the structuralist method, if there is any such thing. After all, any given text is a text with respect to other texts as well: it is the literal expression of a figurally incorporated tradition of textuality. What is not the literal expression of another literally understandable piece of language is at most analogically equivalent. Our contention is that the way to discover these analogies is regulated by the problematological method. Any isolated text is related to *problems* which can be found in other texts, albeit dealt with differently due to its different place within society and history. This cross-sectional analysis does not prevent the questioner from considering any given text as a problematic in itself which deserves to be questioned independently of all others that could be deemed to be related to it on some ground or other. The manner according to which one gives an interpretation of an event or a fact, i.e. its symbolic nature, depends upon the way one sees the text as a whole. The death of a character in a novel, for example, will mean different things, besides being a death, as a function of the problematic one affirms to be at play in the text. It is the problem which highlights the symbolic value of facts or dialogues, and not the reverse.

On the other hand, the link between two texts, even when some given problem makes this link, cannot serve as a pretext for neglecting the deeper reasons that lead that problem to be treated in both texts. Structuralism neglects history, problematology cannot afford to do so.

FOOTNOTES

1. "To compose the *Quixote* at the beginning of the XVIIth Century was a reasonable undertaking, and perhaps even unavoidable; at the beginning of the XXth, it is almost impossible." (Borges 1970: 68)

2. "The contradiction in style is also vivid. The archaic style of Ménard – quite foreign after all – suffers from a certain affectation. Not so that of his forerunner, who handles with ease the current Spanish of his time." (Borges 1970: 69)

3. This latter consequence has been denied by linguists, like Chomsky in his context-free approach. However, in this approach, sentences are still studied in isolation, and language is not envisaged as a flow of discourse, which is more akin to the real, everyday practice of language. Understanding, in the New Grammar, does not depend any longer on the inner structure of the sentence, but on some innate capacity of the subject to produce and grasp such an *a priori* structure. I do not really know whether this change contributes anything to the understanding of understanding since the single sentence remains the unit. As to our innate deep-structuring activity, if it exists at all, it is as *ad hoc* as it can be.

4. They are, at any rate, logically substitutable, even when they differ in their linguistic appearance.

5. For a fully articulated version of this conception of language, see Meyer (1979b, 1981, 1982).

6. One could deny that (1), (2), and (3) are actually equivalent, and that (1) would be the meaning of (2), let alone of (3). The source of this contention reflects the fact that they answer different questions, though (1) answers all those answered by (2), and (2) all those answered by (3). It is only when the question answered is specified that (1) and (2), for instance, are perfectly substitutable. This is a serious restriction on Frege's views and on componential analysis in general, since it supports the question view instead.

7. For instance, if somebody says *I have nothing personal against Mr. X*, it is because the addressee could have thought the opposite. The question of personal enmity is then raised by that very sentence and since the possibility of such a feeling has been alluded to, the suspicion that the speaker could still, in fact, be concealing enmity is also raised by his denegation. This can be generalized: whatever we say raises a question.

8. By 'pragmatically', I mean that the substitution is not *literally* equivalent, but that it is *figuratively* so.

9. Means = can be rendered by = is equivalent to = says that = implies = gives as a problem = is. In one sense, *It is one o'clock* means as statement between quotes 'I'm hungry ...' *If you know the speaker's problem, you know what is meant by (9).*

10. If, for example, I write to someone who made me an offer a few months earlier and say *If your proposal still holds,* ... , my explicit answer contains a question which is thereby raised, namely that the proposal may not hold anymore. This implied question could give my addressee an argument for taking back his offer. If I had not raised the question by saying all that, I would have prevented my addressee from reacting dialectically. The question of that possible dialogue would never have been alluded to.

11. Let us note, in passing, that this is a feature of many ordinary situations, of all debates on ethical values, and as we shall see, of literature too.

12. I call them intensifiers since, as we shall see, all sentences naturally (i.e. contextually) have a rhetorical-argumentative impact.

13. Granger (1968) defines style as "the individual solution brought to the difficulties that any problem of structuring raises".

14. A good example is given by Yeats's poem, cited in de Man (1979).

15. "Roland Barthes uses the term 'hermeneutic' to describe this function, which 'articulates in various ways a question, its response and the variety of chance events which can either formulate the question or delay the answer.' [Barthes 1970: 17] 'What will happen?' is the basic question." (Chatman 1978: 48) Chatman, in that same book, stresses the fact that, in modern plots, it is not so much questions which are involved, but time relations. But it seems clear to me that conventional temporal order serves the same purpose: it links a beginning (of what?) and an end (to what?) which are to be defined with regard to a problematic, illustrated by the succession of narrated events.

16. Hence the distinction that has been made between being and appearances, the latter word is *phainomenon* in Greek.

17. The primary feature of our human mind is that our relationship to the visible can only take place through the mediation of those invisible entities called concepts (Kant, Heidegger, and Merleau-Ponty have re-emphasized this point).

18. Heidegger has brilliantly shown that ideas are the necessary 'instruments' of our vision. They render it possible and necessary to relate to objects *empirically*. Indeed, in view of our 'forgetfulness of being', ideas are what enables us to conceive objects in the first place, that is, to conceptualize them in terms of empiricalness. Being will henceforth have to be seen, touched, etc. and be expressed in and through entities.

19. Meno's Paradox (*Meno* 80 d-e) is well-known: knowledge cannot be expounded, and therefore cannot be developed or occur at all through questioning. If I know what I am looking for, there is no need to look for it; if I do not know what to look for, how could I ever succeed in attaining the answer? In other words, questioning is either a useless or an impossible method of acquiring any knowledge.

20. Those three main criticisms have been treated in Meyer (1979a).

21. As for Aristotle, he studied questions a little more than Plato, but only to confine them to dialectic, which, contrary to Plato's dialectic, is not constitutive of science.

22. We label *a religious creed* an idea that in itself represents a whole ideology, materialized by the ideas that mediation between the human and the divine is necessary, that the gods cause natural phenomena, hence that certain rituals are necessary for causing these phenomena, etc.

23. The proposition q in question is either rejected or accepted, but is not discovered.

24. They are answers with respect to 'infrastructural problems'. When will scientists realize that the nature of the relationship between the so-called 'social base' and its various ideological expressions is not mechanical but rather ought to be seen as a problem-answer complex, which must then be elucidated in the light of problematology.

25. See also Iser (1975a, b). The issue of ideology is also developed in Enzensberger (1981).

26. "It is an old idea that the more pointedly and logically we formulate a thesis, the more irresistibly it cries out for its antithesis." (Hesse 1972: 1)

27. The shaman of our example neither supports some basic idea nor defends it as such. He can give an answer on the basis of his ideology without having to assume, or even question, that it is an ideology and that its claims could be questioned.

28. The term *ideological problem* does not refer to a problem that is only an idea. On the contrary, it denotes reality itself which is always problematic for an ideology. An ideological problem is not an internal deficiency but rather the result of the constant confrontation of ideas with the real. It is the real as external and alien to our ideas.

29. For further developments, see Köhler (1970: 5-36).

30. "The epic hero is, strictly speaking, never an individual" (Lukàcs 1978: 66).

31. A similar example can be found when the knight takes a flock of sheep for an army (Cervantes 1950: I, 139).

32. This is also one of the ideas in Hesse's *The glass bead game*, with which *Don Quixote* can be compared.

33. The use of a principle, like Frege's principle of composition, belongs to this category, not because the principle itself is an automatism, but simply because we can allegedly apply a rule like Frege's quite mechanically.

34. And, as we know from tradition itself, understanding has often, if not always, been associated with these enigmatic notions. This is apparently still the case. Hermeneutics, for Eliade, is a procedure that must necessarily rely on intuition and revelation, because we have lost the sense of what should always have remained evident (cf. Marino 1981: 57).

35. See also Jauss (1976).

REFERENCES

Alberes, R.M.
    1966   Les métamorphoses du roman. Paris: Albin Michel.

Apel, K.-O.
    1980   "Intentions, conventions, and reference to things". In J. Bouveresse and H.
              Parret (eds.), Meaning and Understanding. Berlin: Walter de Gruyter, 79-111.

Bakhtin, M.
    1978   Esthétique et théorie du roman. Paris: Gallimard.

Barthes, R.
    1964   Le degré zéro de l'écriture. Paris: Gonthier.

    1970   S/Z. Paris: Le Seuil.

Barthes, R. (ed.)
    1981   Analyse structurale des récits. Paris: Le Seuil.

Booth, W.
    1961   The rhetoric of fiction. Chicago: University of Chicago Press.

Borges, J.L.
    1970   Labyrinths. Harmondsworth: Penguin Books.

Cervantes, M.
    1950   Don Quixote, translated by J.M. Cohen. Harmondsworth: Penguin Books.

Chatman, S.
    1978   Story and discourse. Ithaca: Cornell University Press.

Cohen, R.
    1978   "Remarks of formalist and hermeneutic features". In M. Valdés and O.J.
              Miller (eds.), Interpretation of narrative. Toronto: University of Toronto
              Press, 3-7.

Culler, J.
    1975   Structuralist poetics. Ithaca: Cornell University Press.

    1981   The pursuit of signs. Ithaca: Cornell University Press.

de Man, P.
    1979   "Semiology and Rhetoric". In J. Harari (ed.), Textual strategies. Ithaca:
              Cornell University Press, 121-140. (Final version in P. de Man, Allegories of
              reading. New Haven/London: Yale University Press, 3-19.)

Dubois, J., F. Edeline, J.M. Klinkenberg, P. Minguet, F. Pire, and H. Trinon
    1970   Rhétorique générale. Paris: Larousse.

Eco, U.
  1976   Opera aperta. Milano: Bompiani.

  1979   Lector in fabula. Milano: Bompiani.

Ellis, J.
  1974   The theory of literary criticism. Berkeley: The University of California Press.

Enzensberger, C.
  1981   Literatur und Interesse. Frankfurt: Suhrkamp.

Frank, M.
  1980   Das Sagbare und das Unsagbare. Frankfurt: Suhrkamp.

Frege, G.
  1970   Philosophical writings. Oxford: Basil Blackwell.

Frye, N.
  1957   The anatomy of criticism. Princeton: Princeton University Press.

Gadamer, H.-G.
  1975a   Truth and method. London: Sheed and Ward.

  1975b   "Wirkungsgeschichte und Applikation". In R. Warning (ed.), 113-125.

Goody, E.
  1978   Questions and politeness. Cambridge: Cambridge University Press.

Granger, G.-G.
  1968   Essai d'une philosophie du style. Paris: Armand Colin.

Hamburger, K.
  1973   The logic of literature. Bloomington: Indiana University Press.

Hesse, H.
  1972   The glass bead game (Magister ludi). Harmondsworth: Penguin Books.

Hirsch, E.D.
  1967   Validity in interpretation. New Haven: Yale University Press.

Holland, N.
  1975   The dynamics of literary response. New York: Norton.

Iser, W.
  1975a   "Die Wirklichkeit der Fiktion". In R. Warning (ed.), 300-311.

  1975b   "The reality of fiction". New Literary History 7.7-38.

  1978   The act of reading. Baltimore: The John Hopkins University Press. (Translation of W. Iser, Der Akt des Lesens. München: Fink.)

Jauss, H.R.
  1976   "Goethes und Valérys *Faust*: Zur Hermeneutik von Frage und Antwort". Comparative Literature 28.201-232.

  1978   Pour une esthétique de la réception. Paris: Gallimard. (English translation: H.R. Jauss, 1982 Towards an aesthetics of reception, translated by T. Bahti. Minneapolis: University of Minnesota Press.)

Juhl, P.D.
1980   Interpretation. Princeton: Princeton University Press.

Köhler, E.
1970   Ideal und Wirklichkeit in der höfischen Epik. Tübingen: Niemeyer.

Laurent, J.
1977   Le roman du roman. Paris: Gallimard.

Levi-Strauss, C.
1972   Le cru et le cuit. Plon: Paris.

Lukács, G.
1978   The theory of the novel. London: The Merlin Press.

Lyons, J.
1968   Introduction to theoretical linguistics. Cambridge: Cambridge University Press.

Marino, A.
1981   L'herméneutique de Mircea Eliade. Paris: Gallimard.

Meyer, M.
1979a   Découverte et justification en science. Paris: Klincksieck.

1979b   "Dialectique, rhétorique, herméneutique et questionnement". Revue Internationale de Philosophie 127/128.145-177.

1980   "Dialectic and questioning: Socrates and Plato". American Philosophical Quarterly 17:4.281-289.

1981   "La conception problématologique du langage". Langue française 52.80-99.

1982   "Argumentation in the light of a theory of questioning". Philosophy and Rhetoric 15.81-103.

Ortega Y Gasset, J.
1981   Meditaciones del Quijote. Madrid: Revista de Occidente.

Perelman, C. and L. Olbrechts-Tyteca
1969   The new rhetoric. Notre Dame, Ind.: University of Notre Dame Press.

Propp, W.
1965   Morphologie du conte. Paris: Le Seuil.

Ricoeur, P.
1975   La métaphore vive. Paris: Le Seuil.

Riffaterre, M.
1979   Semiotics of poetry. London: Methuen.

Robert, M.
1976   Roman des origines et origines du roman. Paris: Gallimard.

Schlovski, V.
1973   Sur la théorie de la prose. Lausanne: L'âge d'homme.

Scholes, R.
   1974   Structuralism in literarture. New Haven: Yale University Press.

Scholes, R. and R. Kellogg
   1966   The nature of narrative. New York: Oxford University Press.

Stanzel, F.
   1979   Theorie des Erzählens. Göttingen: Vandenhoeck, UTB.

Stierle, K.-H.
   1980   "The reading of fictional texts". In S. Suleiman and I. Corsman (eds.), The
               reader in the text. Princeton: Princeton University Press, 83-105.

Tompkins, J. (ed.)
   1980   Reader-response. Baltimore: The Johns Hopkins Press.

Warning, R. (ed.)
   1975   Rezeptionsästhetik. München: Fink, UTB.

Wiesenthal, L.
   1979   "Ästhetische Erklärung". In U. Nassen (ed.), Studien zur materialen Herme-
               neutik. München: Fink, UTB, 62-100.

In the PRAGMATICS & BEYOND series the following monographs have been published thus far:

I:1.   *Anca: M. Nemoianu*: The Boat's Gonna Leave: A Study of Children Learning a Second Language from Conversations with Other Children.
Amsterdam, 1980, vi, 116 pp. Paperbound.

I:2.   *Michael D. Fortescue*: A Discourse Production Model for 'Twenty Questions'.
Amsterdam, 1980, x, 137 pp. Paperbound.

I:3.   *Melvin Joseph Adler*: A Pragmatic Logic for Commands.
Amsterdam, 1980, viii, 131 pp. Paperbound.

I:4.   *Jef Verschueren*: On Speech Act Verbs.
Amsterdam, 1980, viii, 83 pp. Paperbound.

I:5.   *Geoffrey N. Leech*: Explorations in Semantics and Pragmatics.
Amsterdam, 1980, viii, 133 pp. Paperbound.

I:6.   *Herman Parret*: Contexts of Understanding.
Amsterdam, 1980, viii, 109 pp. Paperbound.

I:7.   *Benoît de Cornulier*: Meaning Detachment.
Amsterdam, 1980, vi, 124 pp. Paperbound.

I:8.   *Peter Eglin*: Talk and Taxonomy: A methodological comparison of ethnosemantics and ethnomethodology with reference to terms for Canadian doctors.
Amsterdam, 1980, x, 125 pp. Paperbound.

II:1.   *John Dinsmore*: The Inheritance of Presupposition.
Amsterdam, 1980, vi, 116 pp. Paperbound.

II:2.   *Charles Travis*: The True and the False: The Domain of the Pragmatic.
Amsterdam, 1980, vi, 116 pp. Paperbound.

II:3.   *Johan Van der Auwera*: What do we talk about when we talk? Speculative grammar and the semantics and pragmatics of focus.
Amsterdam, 1980, vi, 116 pp. Paperbound.

II:4.   *Joseph F. Kess & Ronald A. Hoppe*: Ambiguity in Psycholinguistics.
Amsterdam, 1980, vi, 116 pp. Paperbound.

II:5.   *Karl Sornig*: Lexical Innovation: A study of slang, colloquialisms and casual speech.
Amsterdam, 1980, vi, 116 pp. Paperbound.

II:6.   *Knud Lambrecht*: Topic, Antitpoic and Verb Agreement in Non-Standard French.
Amsterdam, 1980, vi, 116 pp. Paperbound.

II:7.   *Jan-Ola Östman*: 'You Know': A discourse-functional study.
Amsterdam, 1980, vi, 116 pp. Paperbound.

II:8.   *Claude Zilberberg*: Essai sur les modalités tensives.
Amsterdam, 1980, vi, 116 pp. Paperbound.

III:1.   *Ivan Fonagy*: Situation et signification.
Amsterdam, 1980, vi, 116 pp. Paperbound.

III:2/3. *Jürgen Weissenborn and Wolfgang Klein (eds.)*: Here and There. Cross-linguistic Studies in Deixis and Demonstration.
Amsterdam, 1982. vi, 296 pp. Paperbound.

III:4.   *Waltraud Brennenstuhl*: Control and Ability. Towards a Biocybernetics of Language.
Amsterdam, 1982. vi, 123 pp. Paperbound.

III:5.   *Wolfgang Wildgen*: Catastrophe Theoretic Semantics. An Elaboration and Application of René Thom's Theory.
Amsterdam, 1982. iv, 124 pp. Paperbound.

III:6.   *René Dirven, Louis Goossens, Yvan Putseys and Emma Vorlat*: The Scene of Linguistic Action and its Perspectivization by SPEAK, TALK, SAY and TELL.
Amsterdam, 1982. vi, 186 pp. Paperbound.

III:7.   *Thomas Ballmer*: Biological Foundations of Linguistic Communication. Towards a Biocybernetics of Language.
Amsterdam, 1982. x, 161 pp. Paperbound.

III:8.   *Douglas N. Walton*: Topical Relevance in Argumentation.
Amsterdam, 1982. viii, 81 pp. Paperbound.

IV:1.   *Marcelo Dascal*: Pragmatics and the Philosophy of Mind. Vol. I.
Amsterdam, 1983. xii, 198 pp. + Index. Paperbound.

IV:2.   *Richard Zuber*: Non-declarative Sentences.
Amsterdam, 1983. ix, 123 pp. Paperbound.

IV:3.   *Michel Meyer*: Meaning and Reading. A Philosophical Essay on Language and Literature.
Amsterdam, 1983. ix, 176 pp. Paperbound.

IV:4.   *Walburga von Raffler-Engel*: The Perception of Nonverbal behavior in the career interview.
Amsterdam, 1983. viii, 148 pp. Paperbound.

IV:5.   *Jan Prucha*: Pragmalinguistics: East European Approaches.
Amsterdam, 1983. 120 pp. Paperbound.

IV:6.   *Alex Huebler*: Understatements and Hedges in English.
Amsterdam, 1983. 120 pp. Paperbound.

IV:7.   *Herman Parret*: Semiotics and Pragmatics. An Evaluative Comparison of Conceptual Frameworks.
Amsterdam, 1983. xii, 136 pp. Paperbound.

IV:8.   *Jürgen Streeck*: Social Order in Child Communication. A Study in Microethnography.
Amsterdam, 1983. 120 pp. Paperbound.